ALICE
SIT-BY-THE-FIRE

J. M. Barrie

New York, C. Scribner's sons, 1920.

Contents

ALICE SIT-BY-THE-FIRE
BY
J. M. BARRIE

THE PLAYS OF J. M. BARRIE

ALICE SIT-BY-THE-FIRE
I

ONE would like to peep covertly into Amy's diary (octavo, with the word 'Amy' in gold letters wandering across the soft brown leather covers, as if it was a long word and, in Amy's opinion, rather a dear). To take such a liberty, and allow the reader to look over our shoulders, as they often invite you to do in novels (which, however, are much more coquettish things than plays) would be very helpful to us; we should learn at once what sort of girl Amy is, and why to-day finds her washing her hair. We should also get proof or otherwise, that we are interpreting her aright; for it is our desire not to record our feelings about Amy, but merely Amy's feelings about herself; not to tell what we think happened, but what Amy thought happened. The book, to be sure, is padlocked, but we happen to know where it is kept. (In the lower drawer of that hand-painted escritoire.) Sometimes in the night Amy, waking up, wonders whether she did lock her diary, and steals downstairs in white to make sure. On these occasions she undoubtedly lingers among the pages, re-reading the peculiarly delightful bit she wrote yesterday; so we could peep over her shoulder, while the reader peeps over ours. Then why don't we do it? Is it because this would be a form of eavesdropping, and that we cannot be sure our hands are clean enough to turn the pages of a young girl's thoughts? It cannot be that, because the novelists do it. It is because in a play we must tell nothing that is not revealed by the spoken words; you must find out all you want to know from them; there is no weather even in plays nowadays except in melodrama; the novelist can have sixteen chapters about the hero's grandparents, but we cannot even say he had any unless he says it himself. There can be no rummaging in the past for us to show what sort of people our characters are; we are allowed only to present them as they toe the mark; then the handkerchief falls, and off they go.

So now we know why we must not spy into Amy's diary. Perhaps we have not always been such sticklers for the etiquette of the thing; but we are always sticklers on Thursdays, and this is a Thursday.

As you are to be shown Amy's room, we are permitted to describe it, though not to tell (which would be much more interesting) why a girl of seventeen has, as her very own, the chief room of a house. The moment you open the door of this room (and please, you are not to look consciously at the escritoire as if you knew the diary was in it) you are aware, though Amy may not be visible, that there is an uncommonly clever girl in the house. The door does not always open easily, because attached thereto is a curtain which frequently catches in it, and this curtain is hand-sewn (extinct animals); indeed a gifted woman's touch is everywhere; if you are not hand-sewn you are almost certainly hand-painted, but incompletely, for Amy in her pursuit of the arts has often to drop one in order to keep pace with another. Some of the chairs have escaped as yet, but their time will come. The table-cover and the curtains are of a lovely pink, perforated ingeniously with many tiny holes, which when you consider them against a dark background, gradually assume the appearance of something pictorial, such as a basket of odd flowers. The fender stool is in brown velvet, and there are words on it that invite you to sit down. Some of the letters of this message have been burned away. There are artistic white bookshelves hanging lopsidedly here and there, and they also have pink curtains, no larger than a doll's garments. These little curtains are for covering the parts where there are no books as yet. The pictures on the walls are mostly studies done at school, and include the well-known windmill, and the equally popular old lady by the shore. Their frames are of fir-cones, glued together, or of straws which have gone limp, and droop like streaks of macaroni. There is a cosy corner; also a milking-stool, but no cow. The lampshades have had ribbons added to them, and from a distance look like ladies of the ballet. The flower-pot also is in a skirt. Near the door is a large screen, such as people hide behind in the more ordinary sort of play; it will be interesting to see whether we can resist the temptation to hide some one behind it.

A few common weeds rear their profane heads in this innocent garden; for instance a cruet-stand, a basket of cutlery, and a triangular dish of the kind in which the correct confine cheese. They have not strayed here, they live here; indeed this is among other things the dining- room of a modest little house in Brompton made beautiful, or nearly so, by a girl, who has a soul above food and conceals its accessories as far as possible from view, in drawers, even in the waste-paper basket. Not a dish, not a spoon, not a fork, is hand-painted, a sufficient indication of her contempt for them.

Amy is present, but is not seen to the best advantage, for she has been washing her hair, and is now drying it by the fire. Notable among her garments are a dressing-jacket and a towel, and her head is bent so far back over the fire that we see her face nearly upside-down. This is no position in which we can do justice to her undoubted facial charm. Seated near her is her brother Cosmo, a boy of thirteen, in naval uniform. Cosmo is a cadet at Osborne, and properly proud of his station, but just now he looks proud of nothing. He is plunged in gloom. The cause of his woe is a telegram, which he is regarding from all points of the compass, as if in hopes of making it send him better news. At last he gives expression to his feelings. 'All I can say,' he sums up in the first words of the play, 'is that if father tries to kiss me, I shall kick him.'

If Amy makes any reply the words arrive upside-down and are unintelligible. The maid announces Miss Dunbar. Then Amy rises, brings her head to the position in which they are usually carried; and she and Ginevra look into each other's eyes. They always do this when they meet, though they meet several times a day, and it is worth doing, for what they see in those pellucid pools is love eternal. Thus they loved at school (in their last two terms), and thus they will love till the grave encloses them. These thoughts, and others even more beautiful, are in their minds as they gaze at each other now. No man will ever be able to say

'Amy,' or to say 'Ginevra,' with such a trill as they are saying it.

'Ginevra, my beloved.'

'My Amy, my better self.'

'My other me.'

There is something almost painful in love like this.

'Are you well, Ginevra?'

'Quite well, Amy.'

Heavens, the joy of Amy because Ginevra is quite well.

'How did my Amy sleep?'

'I had a good night.'

How happy is Ginevra because Amy has had a good night. All this time they have been slowly approaching each other, drawn by a power stronger than themselves. Their intention is to kiss. They do so. Cosmo snorts, and betakes himself to some other room, his bedroom probably, where a man may be alone with mannish things, his razor, for instance. The maidens do not resent his rudeness. They know that poor Cosmo's time will come, and they are glad to be alone, for they have much to say that is for no other mortal ears. Some of it is sure to go into the diary; indeed if we were to put our ear to the drawer where the diary is we could probably hear its little heart ticking in unison with theirs.

It is Ginevra who speaks first. She is indeed the bolder of the two. She grips Amy's hand and says quite firmly, 'Amy, shall we go to *another* to-night?' This does not puzzle Amy, she is prepared for it, her honest grey eyes even tell that she has wanted it, but now that it is come she quails a little. 'Another theatre?' she murmurs. 'Ginevra, that would be five in one week.'

Ginevra does not blanch. 'Yes,' she says recklessly, 'but it is also only eight in seventeen years.'

'Isn't it,' says Amy, comforted. 'And they have taught us so much, haven't they? Until Monday, dear, when we went to our first real play we didn't know what Life is.'

'We were two raw, unbleached school-girls, Amy--absolutely unbleached.'

It is such a phrase as this that gives Ginevra the moral ascendancy in their discussions.

'Of course,' Amy ventures, looking perhaps a little unbleached even now, 'of course I had my diary, dear, and I do think that, even before Monday, there were things in it of a not wholly ordinary kind.'

'Nothing,' persists Ginevra cruelly, 'that necessitated your keeping it locked.'

'No, I suppose not,' sadly enough. 'You are quite right, Ginevra. But we have made up for lost time. Every night since Monday, including the matinee, has been a revelation.'

She closes her eyes so that she may see the revelations more clearly. So does Ginevra.

'Amy, that heart-gripping scene when the love-maddened woman visited the *man in his chambers*.'

'She wasn't absolutely love-maddened, Ginevra; she really loved her husband best all the time.'

'Not till the last act, darling.'

'Please don't say it, Ginevra. She was most foolish, especially in the crepe de chine, but *we* know that she only went to the man's chambers to get back her letters. How I trembled for her then.'

'I was strangely calm,' says Ginevra the stony hearted.

'Oh, Ginevra, I had such a presentiment that the husband

would call at those chambers while she was there. And he did. Ginevra, you remember his knock upon the door. Surely you trembled then?'

Ginevra knits her lips triumphantly.

'Not even then, Amy. Somehow I felt sure that in the nick of time her lady friend would step out from somewhere and say that the letters were *hers*.'

'Nobly compromising herself, Ginevra.'

'Amy, how I love that bit where she says so unexpectedly, with noble self-renunciation, "He is my affianced husband."'

'Isn't it glorious. Strange, Ginevra, that it happened in each play.'

'That was because we always went to the thinking theatres, Amy. Real plays are always about a lady and two men; and alas, only one of them is her husband. That is Life, you know. It is called the odd, odd triangle.'

'Yes, I know.' Appealingly, 'Ginevra, I hope it wasn't wrong of me to go. A month ago I was only a school-girl.'

'We both were.'

'Yes, but you are now an art student, in lodgings, with a latch-key of your own; you have no one dependent on you, while I have a brother and sister to--to form.'

'You must leave it to the Navy, dear, to form Cosmo, if it can; and as the sister is only a baby, time enough to form her when she can exit from her pram.'

'I am in a mother's place for the time being, Ginevra.'

'Even mothers go to thinking theatres.'

'Whether mine does, Ginevra, I don't even know. This is a very strange position I am in, awaiting the return from India of parents I have not seen since I was twelve years old. I don't even know if they will like the house. The rent is what they told me to give, but perhaps my scheme of decoration won't appeal to them; they may think my housekeeping has been defective, and may not make allowance for my being so new to it.'

Ginevra takes Amy in her arms. 'My ownest Amy, if they are not both on their knees to you for the noble way in which you have striven to prepare this house for them--'

'Darling Ginevra, all I ask is to be allowed to do my duty.'

'Listen, then, Amy: your duty is to be able to help your parents in every way when they return. Your mother having been so long in India can know little about Life; how sweet, then, for you to be able to place your knowledge at her feet.'

'I had thought of that, dearest.'

'Then Amy, it would be simply wrong of us not to go to another theatre to-night. I have three and ninepence, so that if you can scrape together one and threepence--'

'Generous girl, it can't be.'

'Why not, Amy?'

The return of Cosmo handling the telegram more pugnaciously than ever provides the answer.

'Cosmo, show Miss Dunbar the telegram.'

Miss Dunbar reads: 'Boat arrived Southampton this morning.'

'A day earlier than they expected,' Amy explains.

'It's the other bit I am worrying about,' Cosmo says darkly. The other bit proves to be 'Hope to reach our pets this afternoon. Kisses from both to all. Deliriously excited. Mummy and Dad.'

Now we see why Cosmo has been in distress.

'Pets, kisses,' he cries. 'What can the telegraph people think.'

'Surely,' Amy says, 'you want to kiss your mother.'

'I'm going to kiss her,' he replies stoutly. 'I mean to do it. It's father I am worrying about; with his "kisses to *both from all*." All I can say is that, if father comes slobbering over me, I'll surprise him.'

Here the outer door slams, and the three start to their feet as if Philippi had dawned. To Cosmo the slam sounds uncommonly like a father's kiss. He immediately begins to rehearse the greeting which is meant to ward off the fatal blow. 'How are you, father? I'm glad to see you, father; it's a long journey from India; won't you sit down?'

Amy is the first to recover. 'How silly of us,' she says; 'it is only nurse with baby.'

Presumably what we hear is a perambulator backing into its stall in the passage. Then nurse is distinctly heard in the adjoining room, and we may gather that this is for the nonce the nursery of the house, though to most occupants it would be the back dining-room. There is a door between the two rooms, and Cosmo, peeping through a chink in it, sounds to his fellow-conspirators the All's Well.

'Poor nurse,' Amy says with a kind sigh, 'I suppose I had better show her the telegram. She is sure to cry. She looks upon mother as a thief who has come to steal baby from her.'

Ginevra wags her head to indicate that this is another slice of Life; and nurse being called in is confronted with the telegram. She runs a gamut of emotion without words, implies that she is nobody and must submit, nods humbly, sets her teeth, is both indignant and servile, and finally bursts into tears. Amy tries to comfort her, but gets this terrible answer: 'They'll be bringing a black woman to nurse her--a yah-yah they call them.'

Amy signs to Ginevra, and Ginevra signs to Amy. These two souls perfectly understand each other, and the telegraphy means that it will be better for dear Ginevra to retire for a time to dear Amy's sweet little bedroom. Amy slips the diary into the hand of Ginevra, who pops upstairs with it to read the latest instalment. Nurse rambles on. 'I have had her for seventeen months. She was just two months old, the angel, when they sent her to England, and she has been mine ever since. The most of them has one look for their mammas and one look for their nurse, but she knew no better than to have both looks for me.' She returns to the nursery, wailing 'My reign is over.'

'Do you think Molly *will* chuck nurse for mother?' asks Cosmo, to whom this is a new thought.

'It is the way of children,' the more experienced Amy tells him.

'Shabby little beasts,' the man says.

'You mustn't say that, Cosmo; but still it is hard on nurse. Of course,' with swimming eyes, 'in a sense it's hard on all of us--I mean to be expecting parents in these circumstances. There must be almost the same feeling of strangeness in the house as when it is a baby that is expected.'

'I suppose it is a bit like that,' Cosmo says gloomily. He goes to her as the awfulness of this sinks into him: 'Great Scott, Amy, it can't be quite so bad as that.'

Amy, who is of a very affectionate nature, is glad to have the comfort of his hand.

'What do we really know about mother, Cosmo?' she says

darkly.

They are perhaps a touching pair.

'There are her letters, Amy.'

'Can one know a person by letters? Does she know you, Cosmo, by your letters to her, saying that your motto is "Something attempted, something done to earn a night's repose," and so on.'

'Well, I thought that would please her.'

'Perhaps in her letters she says things just to please us.'

Cosmo wriggles.

'This is pretty low of you, damping a fellow when he was trying to make the best of it.'

'All I want you to feel,' Amy says, getting closer to him, 'is that as brother and sister, we are allies, you know--against the unknown.'

'Yes, Amy,' Cosmo says, and gets closer to her.

This so encourages her that she hastens to call him 'dear.'

'I want to say, dear, that I'm very sorry I used to shirk bowling to you.'

'That's nothing. I know what girls are. Amy, it's all right, I really am fond of you.'

'I have tried to be a sort of mother to you, Cosmo.'

'My socks and things--I know.' Returning anxiously to the greater question, 'Amy, do we know anything of them at all?'

'We know some cold facts, of course. We know that father is much older than mother.'

'I can't understand why such an old chap should be so keen to kiss me.'

'Mother is forty,' Amy says in a low voice.

'I thought she was almost more than forty,' Cosmo says in a

still lower voice.

Amy shudders. 'Don't be so ungenerous, Cosmo.' But she has to add. 'Of course we must be prepared to see her look older.'

'Why?'

'She will be rather yellow, coming from India, you know. They will both be a little yellow.'

They exchange forlorn glances, but Cosmo says manfully, 'We shan't be any the less fond of them for that, Amy.'

'No, indeed.'

They clasp hands on it, and Cosmo has an inspiration.

'Do you think we should have these yellow flowers in the room? They might feel--eh?'

'How thoughtful of you, dear. I shall remove them at once. After all, Cosmo, we seem to know a good deal about them; and then we know some other things by heredity.'

'Heredity? That's drink, isn't it?'

She who has been to so many theatres smiles at him. 'No, you boy! It's something in a play. It means that if we know ourselves well, we know our parents also. From thinking of myself, Cosmo, I know mother. In her youth she was one who did not love easily; but when she loved once it was for aye. A nature very difficult to understand, but profoundly interesting. I can feel her *within me*, as she was when she walked down the aisle on that strong arm, to honour and obey him henceforth for aye. What cared they that they had to leave their native land, they were together for aye. And so--' Her face is flushed. Cosmo interrupts selfishly.

'What about father?'

'Very nice, unless you mention rupees to him. You see the pensions of all Indian officers are paid in rupees, which means that for every 2s. due to them they get only 1s. 4d. If you mention rupees to any one of them he flares up like a burning paper.'

'I know. I shall take care. But what would you say he was like by heredity?'

'Quiet, unassuming, yet of an intensely proud nature. One who if he was deceived would never face his fellow-creatures, but would bow his head before the wind and die. A strong man.'

'Do you mean, Amy, that he takes all that from me?'

'I mean that is the sort of man *my* mother would love.'

Cosmo nods. 'Yes, but he is just as likely to kiss me as ever.'

The return of Ginevra makes him feel that this room is no place for him.

'I think,' he says, 'I'll go and walk up and down outside, and have a look at them as they're getting out of the cab. My plan, you see, is first to kiss mother. Then I've made up four things to say to father, and it's after I've said them that the awkward time will come. So then I say, "I wonder what is in the evening papers"; and out I slip, and when I come back you will all have settled down to ordinary life, same as other people. That's my plan.' He goes off, not without hope, and Ginevra shrugs her shoulders forgivingly.

'How strange boys are,' she reflects. 'Have you any "plan," Amy?'

'Only this, dear Ginevra, to leap into my mother's arms.'

Ginevra lifts what can only be called a trouser leg, because that is what it is, though they are very seldom seen alone. 'What is this my busy bee is making?'

'It's a gentleman's leg,' Amy explains, not without a sweet blush. 'You hand-sew them and stretch them over a tin cylinder, and they are then used as umbrella stands. *Art in the Home* says they are all the rage.'

'Oh, Amy, *Boudoir Gossip* says they have quite gone out.'

'Again! Every art decoration I try goes out before I have time to finish it.'

She remembers the diary.

'Did my Ginevra like my new page?'

'Dearest, that is what I came down to speak about. You forgot to give me the key.'

'Ginevra, can you ever forgive me? Let us go up and read it together.'

With arms locked they seek the seclusion of Amy's bedroom. Cosmo rushes in to tell them that there is a suspicious-looking cab coming down the street, but finding the room empty he departs again to reconnoitre. A cab draws up, a bell rings, and soon we hear the voice of Colonel Grey. He can talk coherently to Fanny, he can lend a hand in dumping down his luggage in the passage, he can select from a handful of silver wherewith to pay his cabman: all impossible deeds to his Alice, who would drop the luggage on your toes and cast all the silver at your face rather than be kept another minute from her darlings. 'Where are they?' she has evidently cried just before we see her, and Fanny has made a heartless response, for it is a dejected Alice that appears in the doorway of the room.

'*All* out!' she echoes wofully, 'even--even baby?'

'Yes, ma'am.'

The poor mother, who had entered the house like a whirlwind, subsides into a chair. Her arms fall empty by her side: a moment ago she had six of them, a pair for each child. She cries a little, and when Alice cries, which is not often for she is more given to laughter, her face screws up like Molly's rather than like Amy's. She is very unlike the sketch of her lately made by the united fancies of her son and daughter; and she will dance them round the room many times before they know her better. Amy will never be so pretty as her mother, Cosmo will never be so gay, and it will be years before either of them is as young. But it is quite a minute before we suspect this; we must look the other way while the Colonel dries her tears. He is quite a grizzled veteran, and is trying hard to pretend that having done without his children for so many years, a few minutes more is no great matter. His adorable Alice is this man's one joke. Some of those furrows in his brow have come from trying to understand her, he owes the agility of his mind to trying to keep up with her; the humorous twist in his mouth is the result of chuckling over her.

She flutters across the room. 'Robert,' she says, thrilling. 'I daresay my Amy painted that table.'

'Yes, ma'am, she did,' says Fanny.

'Robert, Amy's table.'

'Yes, but keep cool, memsahib.'

'I suppose, ma'am, I'm to take my orders from you now,' the hard-hearted Fanny inquires.

'I suppose so,' Alice says, so timidly that Fanny is encouraged to be bold.

'The poor miss, it will be a bit trying for her just at first.'

Alice is taken aback.

'I hadn't thought of that, Robert.'

Robert thinks it time to take command.

'Fiddle-de-dee. Bring your mistress a cup of tea, my girl.'

'Yes, sir. Here is the tea-caddy, ma'am. I can't take the responsibility; but this is the key.'

'Robert,' Alice says falteringly. 'I daren't break into Amy's caddy. She mightn't like it. I can wait.'

'Rubbish. Give me the key.' Even Fanny cannot but admire the Colonel as he breaks into the caddy.

'That makes me feel I'm master of my own house already. Don't stare at me, girl, as if I was a housebreaker.'

'I feel that is just what we both are,' his wife says; but as soon as they are alone she cries, 'It's home, home! India done, home begun.'

He is as glad as she.

'Home, memsahib. And we've never had a real one before. Thank God, I'm able to give it you at last.'

She darts impulsively from one object in the room to another.

'Look, these pictures. I'm sure they are all Amy's work. They are splendid.' With perhaps a moment's misgiving, 'Aren't they?'

'I couldn't have done them,' the Colonel says guardedly. He considers the hand-painted curtains. 'She seems to have stopped everything in the middle. Still I couldn't have done them. I expect this is what is called a cosy corner.'

But Alice has found something more precious. She utters little cries of rapture.

'What is it?'

'Oh, Robert, a baby's shoe. My baby.' She presses it to her as if it were a dove. Then she is appalled. 'Robert, if I had met my baby coming along the street I shouldn't have known her from other people's babies.'

'Yes, you would,' the Colonel says hurriedly. 'Don't break

down *now*. Just think, Alice; after to-day, you will know your baby anywhere.'

'Oh joy, joy, joy.'

Then the expression of her face changes to 'Oh woe, woe, woe.'

'What is it now, Alice?'

'Perhaps she won't like me.'

'Impossible.'

'Perhaps none of them will like me.'

'My dear Alice, children always love their mother, whether they see much of her or not. It's an instinct.'

'Who told you that?'

'You goose. It was yourself.'

'I've lost faith in it.'

He thinks it wise to sound a warning note. 'Of course you must give them a little time.'

'Robert, Robert. Not another minute. That's not the way people ever love me. They mustn't think me over first or anything of that sort. If they do I'm lost; they must love me at once.'

'A good many have done that,' Robert says, surveying her quizzically as if she were one of Amy's incompleted works.

'You are not implying, Robert, that I ever--. If I ever did I always told you about it afterwards, didn't I? And I *certainly* never did it until I was sure you were comfortable.'

'You always wrapped me up first,' he admits.

'They were only boys, Robert--poor lonely boys. What are you looking so solemn about, Robert?'

'I was trying to picture you as you will be when you settle down.'

She is properly abashed. 'Not settled down yet--with a girl nearly grown up. And yet it's true; it's the tragedy of Alice Grey.' She pulls his hair. 'Oh, husband, when shall I settle down?'

'I can tell you exactly--in a year from to-day. Alice, when I took you away to that humdrummy Indian station I was already quite a middle-aged bloke. I chuckled over your gaiety, but it gave me lumbago to try to be gay with you. Poor old girl, you were like an only child who has to play alone. When for one month in the twelve we went to--to--where the boys were, it was like turning you loose in a sweet-stuff shop.'

'Robert, darling, what nonsense you do talk.'

He makes rather a wry face. 'I didn't always like it, memsahib. But I knew my dear, and could trust her; and I often swore to myself when I was shaving, "I won't ask her to settle down until I have given her a year in England." A year from to-day, you harum-scarum. By that time your daughter will be almost grownup herself; and it wouldn't do to let her pass you.'

'Robert, here is an idea; she and I shall come of age together. I promise; or I shall try to keep one day in front of her, like the school-mistresses when they are teaching boys Latin. Dearest, you haven't been disappointed in me as a whole, have you? I haven't paid you for all your dear kindnesses to me--in rupees, have I?'

His answer is of no consequence, for at this moment there arrives a direct message from heaven. It comes by way of the nursery, and is a child's cry. The heart of Alice Grey stops beating for several seconds. Then it says, 'My Molly!' The nurse appears, starts, and is at once on the defensive.

NURSE. 'Is it--Mrs. Grey?'

ALICE hastily, 'Yes. Is my--child in there?'

NURSE. 'Yes, ma'am.'

COLONEL, ready to catch her if she falls, 'Alice, be calm.'

ALICE, falteringly, 'May I go in, nurse?'

NURSE, cold-heartedly, 'She's sleeping, ma'am, and I have made it a rule to let her wake up naturally. But I daresay it's a bad rule.'

ALICE, her hands on her heart, 'I'm sure it's a good rule. I shan't wake her, nurse.'

COLONEL, showing the stuff he is made of, 'Gad, I will. It's the least she can do to let herself be wakened.'

ALICE, admiring the effrontery of the man, 'Don't interfere, Robert.'

COLONEL. 'Sleeping? Why, she cried just now.'

NURSE. 'That is why I came out--to see who was making so much noise.'

An implacable woman this, and yet when she is alone with Molly a very bundle of delight.

'I'm vexed when she cries--I daresay it's old-fashioned of me. Not being a yah-yah I'm at a disadvantage.'

ALICE, swelling, 'After all, she is *my* child.'

COLONEL, firmly, 'Come along. Alice,'

ALICE. 'I would prefer to go alone, dear.'

COLONEL. 'All right. But break it to her that I'm kicking my heels outside.'

Alice gets as far as the door. The nurse discharges a last duty.

NURSE. 'You won't touch her, ma'am; she doesn't like to be touched by strangers.'

ALICE. 'Strangers!'

COLONEL. 'Really, nurse.'

ALICE. 'It's quite true.'

NURSE. 'She's an angel if you have the right way with her.'

ALICE. 'Robert, if I shouldn't have the right way with her.'

COLONEL. 'You.'

But the woman has scored again.

ALICE, willing to go on her knees, 'Nurse, what sort of a way does she like from strangers?'

NURSE. 'She's not fond of a canoodlin' way.'

ALICE, faintly, 'Is she not?'

She departs to face her child, and the natural enemy follows her, after giving Colonel Grey a moment in which to discharge her if he dares, that is if he wishes to see his baby wither and die. One may as well say here that nurse weathered this and many another gale, and remained in the house for many years to be its comfort and its curse.

Fanny, with the tea-tray, comes and goes without the Colonel's being aware of her presence. He merely knows that he has waved someone away. The fact is that the Colonel is engrossed in a rather undignified pursuit. He is listening avidly at the nursery door, and is thus discovered by another member of his family who has entered cautiously. This is Master Cosmo, who, observing the tea-tray, has the happy notion of interposing it between himself and his father's possible osculatory intentions. He lifts the tray, and thus armed introduces himself.

COSMO. 'Hullo, father.'

His father leaves the door and strides to him.

COLONEL. 'Is it--it's Cosmo.'

COSMO, with the tray well to the fore, 'I'm awfully glad to see you--it's a long way from India.'

COLONEL. 'Put that down, my boy, and let me get hold of you.'

COSMO, ingratiatingly, 'Have some tea, father.'

COLONEL. 'Put it down.'

Cosmo does so, and prepares for the worst. The Colonel takes both his hands.

'Let's have a look at you. So this is you.'

He waggles his head, well-pleased, while Cosmo backs in a gentlemanly manner.

COSMO, implying that this first meeting is now an affair of the past, 'Has Mother gone to lie down?'

COLONEL. 'Lie down? She's in there.'

Cosmo steals to the nursery door and softly closes it.

'Why do you do that?'

COSMO. 'I don't know. I thought it would be--best.' In a burst of candour, 'This is not the way I planned it, you see.'

COLONEL. 'Our meeting? So you've been planning it. My dear fellow, I was planning it too, and my plan--' He is certainly coming closer.

COSMO, hurriedly, 'Yes, I know. Now that's over--our first meeting, I mean; now we settle down.'

COLONEL. 'Not yet. Come here, my boy.'

He draws him to a chair; he evidently thinks that a father and his boy of thirteen can sit in the same chair. Cosmo is burning to be nice to him, but of course there are limits.

COSMO. 'Look here, father. Of course, you see--ways change. I daresay they did it, when you were a boy, but it isn't done now.'

COLONEL. 'What isn't done, you dear fellow?'

COSMO. 'Oh--well!--and then taking both hands and saying 'Dear fellow'--'It's gone out, you know.'

The Colonel chuckles and forbears. 'I'm uncommon glad you told me, Cosmo. Not having been a father for so long, you see, I'm rather raw at it.'

COSMO, relieved, 'That's all right. You'll soon get the hang of it.'

COLONEL. 'If you could give me any other tips?'

COSMO, becoming confidential, 'Well, there's my beastly name. Of course you didn't mean any harm when you christened me Cosmo, but--I always sign myself "C. Grey"--to make the fellows think I'm Charles.'

COLONEL. 'Do they call you that?'

COSMO. 'Lord, no, they call me Grey.'

COLONEL. 'And do you want me to call you Grey?'

COSMO, magnanimously, 'No, I don't expect that. But I thought that before people, you know, you needn't call me anything. If you want to attract my attention you could just say "Hst!"--like that.'

COLONEL. 'Right you are. But you won't make your mother call you Hst.'

COSMO, sagaciously, 'Oh no--of course women are different.'

COLONEL. 'You'll be very nice to her, Cosmo? She had to pinch and save more than I should have allowed--to be able to send you into the navy. We are poor people, you know.'

COSMO. 'I've been planning how to be nice to her.'

COLONEL. 'Good lad. Good lad.'

Cosmo remembers his conversation with Amy, and thoughtfully hides the 'yellow flowers' behind a photograph. This may be called one of his plans for being nice to mother.

COSMO. 'You don't have your medals here, father?'

COLONEL. 'No, I don't carry them about. But your mother does, the goose. They are not very grand ones, Cosmo.'

COSMO, true blue, 'Yes, they are.'

An awkward silence falls. The Colonel has so much to say that he can only look it. He looks it so eloquently that Cosmo's fears return. He summons the plan to his help.

'I wonder what is in the evening papers. If you don't mind, I'll cut out and get one.'

Before he can cut out, however, Alice is in the room, the picture of distress. No wonder, for even we can hear the baby howling.

ALICE, tragically, 'My baby. Robert, listen; that is how I affect her.'

Cosmo cowers unseen.

COLONEL. 'No, no, darling, it isn't you who have made her cry. She--she is teething. It's her teeth, isn't it?' he barks at the nurse, who emerges looking not altogether woeful. 'Say it's her teeth, woman.'

NURSE, taking this as a reflection on her charge. 'She had her teeth long ago.'

ALICE, the forlorn, 'The better to bite me with.'

NURSE, complacently, 'I don't understand it. She is usually the best-tempered lamb--as you may see for yourself, sir.'

It is an imitation that the Colonel is eager to accept, but after one step toward the nursery he is true to Alice.

COLONEL. 'I *decline* to see her. I refuse to have anything to do with her till she comes to a more reasonable frame of mind.'

The nurse retires, to convey possibly this ultimatum to her charge.

ALICE, in the noblest spirit of self-abnegation, 'Go, Robert. Perhaps she--will like you better.'

COLONEL. 'She's a contemptible child.'

But that nursery door does draw him strongly. He finds himself getting nearer and nearer to it. 'I'll show her,' with a happy pretence that his object is merely to enforce discipline. The forgotten Cosmo pops up again; the Colonel introduces him with a gesture and darts off to his baby.

ALICE, entranced, 'My son!'

COSMO, forgetting all plans, 'Mother!' She envelops him in her arms, worshipping him, and he likes it.

ALICE. 'Oh, Cosmo--how splendid you are.'

COSMO, soothingly, 'That's all right, mother.'

ALICE. 'Say it again.'

COSMO. 'That's all right.'

ALICE. 'No, the other word.'

COSMO. 'Mother.'

ALICE. 'Again.'

COSMO. 'Mother--mother--' When she has come to: 'Are you better now?'

ALICE. 'He is my son, and he is in uniform.'

COSMO, aware that allowances must be made, 'Yes, I know.'

ALICE. 'Are you glad to see your mother, Cosmo?'

COSMO. 'Rather! Will you have some tea?'

ALICE. 'No, no, I feel I can do nothing for the rest of my life but hug my glorious boy.'

COSMO. 'Of course, I have my work.'

ALICE. 'His work! Do the officers love you, Cosmo?'

COSMO, degraded, 'Love me! I should think not.'

ALICE. 'I should like to ask them all to come and stay with us.'

COSMO, appalled, 'Great Scott, mother, you can't do things like that.'

ALICE. 'Can't I? Are you very studious, Cosmo?'

COSMO, neatly, 'My favourite authors are William Shakespeare and William Milton. They are grand, don't you think?'

ALICE. 'I'm only a woman, you see; and I'm afraid they sometimes bore me, especially William Milton.'

COSMO, with relief, 'Do they? Me, too.'

ALICE, on the verge of tears again, 'But not half so much as I bore my baby.'

COSMO, anxious to help her, 'What did you do to her?'

ALICE, appealingly, 'I couldn't help wanting to hold her in my arms, could I, Cosmo?'

COSMO, full of consideration, 'No, of course you couldn't.' He reflects. 'How did you take hold of her?'

ALICE. 'I suppose in some clumsy way.'

COSMO. 'Not like this, was it?'

ALICE, gloomily, 'I dare say.'

COSMO. 'You should have done it this way.'

He very kindly shows her how to carry a baby.

ALICE, with becoming humility, 'Thank you, Cosmo.'

He does not observe the gleam in her eye, and is in the high good humour that comes to any man when any woman asks him to show her how to do anything.

COSMO. 'If you like I'll show you with a cushion. You see this'--scoops it up--'is wrong; but this'--he does a little sleight of hand--'is right. Another way is this, with their head hanging over your shoulder, and you holding on firmly to their legs. You wouldn't think it was comfortable, but they like it.'

ALICE, adoring him. 'I see, Cosmo.' She practises diligently with the cushion. 'First this way--then this.'

COSMO. 'That's first-class. It's just a knack. You'll soon pick it up.'

ALICE, practising on him instead of the cushion, 'You darling boy!'

COSMO. 'I think I hear a boy calling the evening papers.'

ALICE, clinging to him, 'Don't go. There can be nothing in the evening papers about what my boy thinks of his mother.'

COSMO. 'Good lord, no.' He thinks quickly. 'You haven't seen Amy yet. It isn't fair of Amy. She should have been here to take some of it off me.'

ALICE. 'Cosmo, you don't mean that I bore you too!'

He is pained. It is now he who boldly encircles her. But his words, though well meant, are not so happy as his action. 'I love you, mother; and I don't think you're so yellow.'

ALICE, the belle of many stations, 'Yellow?' Her brain reels. 'Cosmo, do you think me plain?'

COSMO, gallantly, 'No, I don't. I'm not one of the kind who judge people by their looks. The soul, you know, is what I judge them by.'

ALICE. 'Plain? Me.'

COSMO, the comforter, 'Of course it's all right for girls to bother about being pretty.' He lures her away from the subject. 'I can tell you a funny thing about that. We had theatricals at Osborne one night, and we played a thing called "The Royal Boots."'

ALICE, clapping her hands, 'I played in that, too, last year.'

COSMO. 'You?'

ALICE. 'Yes. Why shouldn't I?'

COSMO. 'But we did it for fun.'

ALICE. 'So did we.'

COSMO, his views on the universe crumbling, 'You still like fun?'

ALICE. 'Take care, Cosmo.'

COSMO. 'But you're our mother.'

ALICE. 'Mustn't mothers have fun?

COSMO, heavily, 'Must they? I see. You had played the dowager.'

ALICE. 'No, I didn't. I played the girl in the Wellington boots.'

COSMO, blinking, 'Mother, I played the girl in the Wellington boots.'

ALICE, happily, 'My son--this ought to bring us closer together.'

COSMO, who has not yet learned to leave well alone, 'But the reason I did it was that we were all boys. Were there no young ladies where you did it, mother?'

ALICE. 'Cosmo.' She is not a tamed mother yet, and in sudden wrath she flips his face with her hand. He accepts it as a smack. The Colonel foolishly chooses this moment to make his return. He is in high good-humour, and does not observe that two of his nearest relatives are glaring at each other.

COLONEL, purring offensively, 'It's all right now, Alice; she took to me at once.'

ALICE, tartly, 'Oh, did she!'

COLONEL. 'Gurgled at me--pulled my moustache.'

ALICE. 'I hope you got on with our dear son as well.'

COLONEL. 'Isn't he a fine fellow.'

ALICE. 'I have just been smacking his face.' She sits down and weeps, while her son stands haughtily at attention.

COLONEL, with a groan, 'Hst, I think you had better go and get that evening paper.'

Cosmo departs with his flag flying, and the bewildered husband seeks enlightenment.

'Smacked his face. But why, Alice?'

ALICE. 'He infuriated me.'

COLONEL. 'He seems such a good boy.'

ALICE, the lowly, 'No doubt he is. It must be very trying to have me for a mother.'

COLONEL. 'Perhaps you were too demonstrative?'

ALICE. 'I daresay. A woman he doesn't know! No wonder I disgusted him.'

COLONEL. 'I can't make it out.'

ALICE, abjectly, 'It's quite simple. He saw through me at once; so did baby.'

The Colonel flings up his hands. He hears whisperings outside the door. He peeps and returns excitedly.

COLONEL. 'Alice, there's a girl there with Cosmo.'

ALICE, on her feet, with a cry, 'Amy.'

COLONEL, trembling, 'I suppose so.'

ALICE, gripping him, 'Robert, if *she* doesn't love me I shall die.'

COLONEL. 'She will, she will.' But he has grown nervous. 'Don't be too demonstrative, dearest.'

ALICE. 'I shall try to be cold. Oh, Amy, love me.'

Amy comes, her hair up, and is at once in her father's arms. Then she wants to leap into the arms of the mother who craves for her. But Alice is afraid of being too demonstrative, and restrains herself. She presses Amy's hands only.

ALICE. 'It is you, Amy. How are you, dear?' She ventures at last to kiss her. 'It is a great pleasure to your father and me to see you again.'

AMY, damped, 'Thank you, mother----Of course I have been looking forward to this meeting very much also.'

ALICE, shuddering, 'It is very sweet of you to say so.'

'Oh how cold,' they are both thinking, while the Colonel regards them uncomfortably. Amy turns to him. She knows already that there is safe harbourage there.

AMY. 'Would you have known me, father?'

COLONEL. 'I wonder. She's not like you, Alice?'

ALICE. 'No. I used to be demonstrative, Amy----'

AMY, eagerly, 'Were you?'

ALICE, hurriedly, 'Oh, I grew out of it long ago.'

AMY, disappointed but sympathetic, 'The wear and tear of life.'

ALICE, wincing, 'No doubt.'

AMY, making conversation, 'You have seen Cosmo?'

ALICE. 'Yes.'

AMY, with pardonable curiosity, 'What did you think of

him?'

ALICE. 'He--seemed a nice boy----'

AMY, hurt, 'And baby?'

ALICE. 'Yes--oh yes.'

AMY. 'Isn't she fat?'

ALICE. 'Is she?'

The nurse's head intrudes.

NURSE. 'If you please, sir--I think baby wants *you* again.'

The Colonel's face exudes complacency, but he has the grace to falter.

COLONEL. 'What do you think, Alice?'

ALICE, broken under the blow, 'By all means go.'

COLONEL. 'Won't you come also? Perhaps if I am with you--'

ALICE, after giving him an annihilating look, 'No, I--I had quite a long time with her.'

The Colonel tiptoes off to his babe with a countenance of foolish rapture; and mother and daughter are alone.

AMY, wishing her father would come back, 'You can't have been very long with baby, mother.'

ALICE. 'Quite long enough.'

AMY. 'Oh.' Some seconds elapse before she can speak again. 'You will have some tea, won't you?'

ALICE. 'Thank you, dear.' They sit down to a chilly meal.

AMY, merely a hostess, 'Both milk and sugar.'

ALICE, merely a guest, 'No sugar.'

AMY. 'I hope you will like the house, mother.'

ALICE. 'I am sure you have chosen wisely. I see you are artistic.'

AMY. 'The decoration isn't finished. I haven't quite decided what this room is to be like yet.'

ALICE. 'One never can tell.'

AMY, making conversation, 'Did you notice that there is a circular drive to the house?'

ALICE. 'No, I didn't notice.'

AMY. 'That would be because the cab filled it; but you can see it if you are walking.'

ALICE. 'I shall look out for it.' Grown desperate, 'Amy, have you nothing more important to say to me?'

AMY, faltering, 'You mean--the keys? Here they are; all with labels on them. And here are the tradesmen's books. They are all paid up to Wednesday.' She sadly lets them go. They lie disregarded in her mother's lap.

ALICE. 'Is there nothing else?'

AMY, with a flash of pride. 'Perhaps you have noticed that my hair is up?'

ALICE. 'It so took me aback, Amy, when you came into the room. How long have you had it up?'

AMY, with large eyes, 'Not very long. I--I began only to-day.'

ALICE, imploringly, 'Dear, put it down again. You are not grown up.'

AMY, almost sternly, 'I feel I am a woman now.'

ALICE, abject, 'A woman--you? Am I never to know my daughter as a girl!'

AMY. 'You were married before you were eighteen.'

ALICE. 'Ah, but I had no mother. And even at that age I knew the world.'

AMY, smiling sadly, 'Oh, mother, not so well as I know it.'

ALICE, sharply, 'What can you know of the world?'

AMY, shuddering, 'More I hope, mother, than you will ever know.'

ALICE, alarmed, 'My child!' Seizing her: 'Amy, tell me what you know.'

AMY. 'Don't ask me, please. I have sworn not to talk of it.'

ALICE. 'Sworn? To whom?'

AMY. 'To another.'

Alice, with a sinking, pounces on her daughter's engagement finger; but it is unadorned.

ALICE. 'Tell me, Amy, who is that other?'

AMY, bravely, 'It is our secret.'

ALICE. 'Amy, I beg you--'

AMY, a heroic figure, 'Dear mother, I am so sorry I must decline.'

ALICE. 'You defy me.' She takes hold of her daughter's shoulders. 'Amy, you drive me frantic. If you don't tell me at once I shall insist on your father--. Oh, you--'

It is not to be denied that she is shaking Amy when the Colonel once more intrudes.

COLONEL, aghast, 'Good heavens, Alice, again! Amy, what does this mean?'

AMY, as she runs, insulted and in tears, from the room, 'It means, father, that I love *you* very much.'

COLONEL, badgered, 'Won't you explain, Alice?'

ALICE. 'Robert, I am in terror about Amy.'

COLONEL. 'Why?'

ALICE. 'Don't ask me, dear--not now--not till I have spoken

to her again.' She clings to her husband. 'Robert, there can't be anything in it?'

COLONEL. 'If you mean anything wrong with our girl, there isn't, memsahib. What great innocent eyes she has.'

ALICE, eagerly, 'Yes, yes, hasn't she, Robert.'

COLONEL. 'All's well with Amy, dear.'

ALICE. 'Of course it is. It was silly of me--My Amy.'

COLONEL. 'And mine.'

ALICE. 'But she seems to me hard to understand.' With her head on his breast, 'I begin to feel Robert that I should have come back to my children long ago--or I shouldn't have come back at all.'

The Colonel is endeavouring to soothe her when Stephen Rollo is shown in. He is very young--too young to be a villain, too round-faced; but he is all the villain we can provide for Amy. His entrance is less ostentatious than it might be if he knew of the role that has been assigned to him. He thinks indeed (sometimes with a sigh) that he is a very good young man; and the Colonel and Alice (without the sigh) think so too. After warm greetings:

STEVE. 'Alice, I daresay you wish me at Jericho; but it's six months since I saw you, and I couldn't wait till to-morrow.'

ALICE, giving him her cheek, 'I believe there's someone in this house glad to see me at last; and you may kiss me for that, Steve.'

STEVE, who has found the cheek wet, 'You are not telling me they don't adore her?'

COLONEL. 'I can't understand it.'

STEVE. 'But by all the little gods of India, you know, every-one has always adored Alice.'

ALICE, plaintively, 'That's why I take it so ill, Steve.'

STEVE. 'Can I do anything? See here, if the house is upside down and you would like to get rid of the Colonel for an hour or two, suppose he dines with me to-night? I'm dying to hear all the news of the Punjab since I left.'

COLONEL, with an eye on the nursery door, 'No, Steve, I--the fact is--I have an engagement.'

ALICE, vindictively, 'He means he can't leave the baby.'

STEVE. 'It has taken to *him*?'

COLONEL, swaggering, 'Enormously.'

ALICE, whimpering, 'They all have. He has stolen them from me. He has taken up his permanent residence in the nursery.'

COLONEL. 'Pooh, fiddlededee. I shall probably come round to-night to see you after dinner, Steve, and bring memsahib with me. In the meantime--'

ALICE, whose mind is still misgiving her about Amy, 'In the meantime I want to have a word with Steve alone, Robert.'

COLONEL. 'Very good.' Stealing towards the nursery, 'Then I shall pop in here again. How is the tea business prospering in London, Steve? Glad you left India?'

STEVE. 'I don't have half the salary I had in India, but my health is better. How are rupees?'

COLONEL. 'Stop it.' He is making a doll of his handkerchief for the further subjugation of Molly. He sees his happy face in a looking-glass and is ashamed of it. 'Alice, I wish it was you they loved.'

ALICE, with withering scorn, 'Oh, go back to your baby.'

As soon as the Colonel has gone she turns anxiously to Steve.

'Steve, tell me candidly what you think of my girl.'

STEVE. 'But I have never set eyes on her.'

ALICE. 'Oh, I was hoping you knew her well. She goes sometimes to the Deans and the Rawlings--all our old Indian friends--'

STEVE. 'So do I, but we never happened to be there at the same time. They often speak of her though.'

ALICE. 'What do they say?'

STEVE. 'They are enthusiastic--an ideal, sweet girl.'

ALICE, relieved, 'I'm so glad. Now you can go, Steve.'

STEVE. 'It's odd to think of the belle of the Punjab as a mother of a big girl.'

ALICE. 'Don't; or I shall begin to think it's absurd myself.'

STEVE. 'Surely the boy felt the spell.' She shakes her head. 'But the boys always did.'

ALICE, wryly, 'They were older boys.'

STEVE. 'I believe I was the only one you never flirted with.'

ALICE, smiling, 'No one could flirt with you, Steve.'

STEVE, pondering, 'I wonder why.' The problem has troubled him occasionally for years.

ALICE. 'I wonder.'

STEVE. 'I suppose there's some sort of want in me.'

ALICE. 'Perhaps that's it. No, it's because you were always such a good boy.'

STEVE, wincing, 'I don't know. Sometimes when I saw you all flirting I wanted to do it too, but I could never think of how to begin.' With a sigh, 'I feel sure there's something pleasant about it.'

ALICE, 'You're a dear, old donkey, Steve, but I'm glad you

came, it has made the place seem more like home. All these years I was looking forward to home; and now I feel that perhaps it is the place I have left behind me.' The joyous gurgling of Molly draws them to the nursery door; and there they are observed by Amy and Ginevra who enter from the hall. The screen is close to the two girls, and they have so often in the last week seen stage figures pop behind screens that, mechanically as it were, they pop behind this one.

STEVE, who little knows that he is now entering on the gay career, 'Listen to the infant.'

ALICE. 'Isn't it horrid of Robert to get on with her so well. Steve, say Robert's a brute.'

STEVE, as he bids her good afternoon, 'Of course he is; a selfish beast.'

ALICE. 'There's another kiss to you for saying so.' The doomed woman presents her cheek again.

STEVE. 'And you'll come to me after dinner to-night, Alice? Here, I'll leave my card, I'm not half a mile from this street.'

ALICE. 'I mayn't be able to get away. It will depend on whether my silly husband wants to stay with his wretch of a baby. I'll see you to the door. Steve, you're *much* nicer than Robert.'

With these dreadful words she and the libertine go. Amy and Ginevra emerge white to the lips; or, at least, they feel as white as that.

AMY, clinging to the screen for support, 'He kissed her.'

GINEVRA, sternly, 'He called her Alice.'

AMY. 'She is going to his house to-night. An assignation.'

GINEVRA. 'They will be chambers, Amy--they are always chambers. And after dinner, he said--so he's stingy, too. Here is his card: "Mr. Stephen Rollo.'"

AMY. 'I have heard of him. They said he was a nice man.'

GINEVRA. 'The address is Kensington West. That's the new name for West Kensington.'

AMY. 'My poor father. It would kill him.'

GINEVRA, the master mind, 'He must never know.'

AMY. 'Ginevra, what's to be done?'

GINEVRA. 'Thank heaven, we know exactly what to do. It rests with you to save her.'

AMY, trembling, 'You mean I must go--to his chambers?'

GINEVRA, firmly, 'At any cost.'

AMY. 'Evening dress?'

GINEVRA. 'It is always evening dress. And don't be afraid of his Man, dear; they always have a Man.'

AMY. 'Oh, Ginevra.'

GINEVRA. 'First try fascination. You remember how they fling back their cloak--like this, dear. If that fails, threaten him. You must get back the letters. There are always letters.'

AMY. 'If father should suspect and follow? They usually do.'

GINEVRA. 'Then you must sacrifice yourself for her. Does my dearest falter?'

AMY, pressing Ginevra's hand, 'I will do my duty. Oh, Ginevra, what things there will be to put in my diary to-night.'

II

NIGHT has fallen, and Amy is probably now in her bedroom, fully arrayed for her dreadful mission. She says good-bye to her diary--perhaps for aye. She steals from the house--to a very different scene, which (if one were sufficiently daring) would represent a Man's Chambers at Midnight. There is no really valid excuse for shirking this scene, which is so popular that every theatre has it stowed away in readiness; it is capable of 'setting' itself should the stage-hands forget to do so.

It should be a handsome, sombre room in oak and dark red, with sinister easy chairs and couches, great curtains discreetly drawn, a door to enter by, a door to hide by, a carelessly strewn table on which to write a letter reluctantly to dictation, another table exquisitely decorated for supper for two, champagne in an ice-bucket, many rows of books which on close examination will prove to be painted wood (the stage Lotharios not being really reading men). The lamps shed a diffused light, and one of them is slightly odd in construction, because it is for knocking over presently in order to let the lady escape unobserved. Through this room moves occasionally the man's Man, sleek, imperturbable, announcing the lady, the lady's husband, the woman friend who is to save them; he says little, but is responsible for all the

arrangements going right; before the curtain rises he may be con-
ceived trying the lamp and making sure that the lady will not
stick in the door.

That is how it ought to be, that is how Amy has seen it several times in the past week; and now that we come to the grapple
we wish we could give you what you want, for you do want it,
you have been used to it, and you will feel that you are looking
at a strange middle act without it. But Steve cannot have such a
room as this, he has only two hundred and fifty pounds a year,
including the legacy from his aunt. Besides, though he is to be a
Lothario (in so far as we can manage it) he is not at present aware
of this, and has made none of the necessary arrangements; if one
of his lamps is knocked over it will certainly explode; and there
cannot be a secret door without its leading into the adjoining
house. (Theatres keep special kinds of architects to design their
rooms.) There is indeed a little cupboard where his crockery is
kept, and if Amy is careful she might be able to squeeze in there.
We cannot even make the hour midnight; it is eight-thirty, quite
late enough for her to be out alone.

Steve has just finished dinner, in his comfortable lodgings.
He is not even in evening dress, but he does wear a lounge jack-
et, which we devoutly hope will give him a rakish air to Amy's
eyes. He would undoubtedly have put on evening dress if he had
known she was coming. His man, Richardson, is waiting on him.
When we wrote that we deliberated a long time. It has an air,
and with a little low cunning we could make you think to the
very end that Richardson was a male. But if the play is acted and
you go to see it, you would be disappointed. Steve, the wretched
fellow, never had a Man, and Richardson is only his landlady's

slavey, aged about fifteen, and wistful at sight of food. We introduce her gazing at Steve's platter as if it were a fairy tale. Steve has often caught her with this rapt expression on her face, and sometimes, as now, an engaging game ensues.

RICHARDSON, blinking, 'Are you finished, sir?' To those who know the game this means, 'Are you to leave the other chop--the one sitting lonely and lovely beneath the dish-cover?'

STEVE. 'Yes.' In the game this is merely a tantaliser.

RICHARDSON, almost sure that he is in the right mood and sending out a feeler, 'Then am I to clear?'

STEVE. 'No.' This is intended to puzzle her, but it is a move he has made so often that she understands its meaning at once.

RICHARDSON, in entranced giggles, 'He, he, he!'

STEVE, vacating his seat, 'Sit down.'

RICHARDSON. 'Again?'

STEVE. 'Sit down, and clear the enemy out of that dish.'

By the enemy he means the other chop: what a name for a chop. Steve plays the part of butler. He brings her a plate from the little cupboard.

'Dinner is served, madam.'

RICHARDSON, who will probably be a great duchess some day, 'I don't mind if I does have a snack.' She places herself at the table after what she conceives to be the manner of the genteelly gluttonous; then she quakes a little. 'If Missis was to catch me.' She knows that Missis is probably sitting downstairs with her arms folded, hopeful of the chop for herself.

STEVE. 'You tuck in and I'll keep watch.'

He goes to the door to peer over the banisters; it is all part of the game. Richardson promptly tucks in with horrid relish.

RICHARDSON. 'What makes you so good to me, sir?'

STEVE. 'A gentleman is always good to a lady.'

RICHARDSON, preening, 'A lady? Go on.'

STEVE. 'And when I found that at my dinner hour you were subject to growing pains I remembered my own youth. Potatoes, madam?'

RICHARDSON, neatly, 'If quite convenient.'

The kindly young man surveys her for some time in silence while she has various happy adventures.

STEVE. 'Can I smoke, Richardson?'

RICHARDSON. 'Of course you can smoke. I have often seen you smoking.'

STEVE, little aware of what an evening the sex is to give him, 'But have I your permission?'

RICHARDSON. 'You're at your tricks again.'

STEVE, severely, 'Have you forgotten already how I told you a true lady would answer?'

RICHARDSON. 'I minds, but it makes me that shy.' She has, however, a try at it. 'Do smoke, Mr. Rollo, I loves the smell of it.'

Steve lights his pipe; no real villain smokes a pipe.

STEVE. 'Smoking is a blessed companion to a lonely devil like myself.'

RICHARDSON. 'Yes, sir.' Sharply, 'Would you say devil to a real lady, sir?'

Steve, it may be hoped, is properly confused, but here the little idyll of the chop is brought to a close by the tinkle of a bell. Richardson springs to attention.

'That will be the friends you are expecting?'

STEVE. 'I was only half expecting them, but I daresay you are right. Have you finished, Richardson?'

RICHARDSON. 'Thereabouts. Would a real lady lick the bone--in company I mean?'

STEVE. 'You know, I hardly think so.'

RICHARDSON. 'Then I'm finished.'

STEVE, disappearing, 'Say I'll be back in a jiffy. I need brushing, Richardson.'

Richardson, no longer in company, is about to hold a last friendly communion with the bone when there is a knock at the door, followed by the entrance of a mysterious lady. You could never guess who the lady is, so we may admit at once that it is Miss Amy Grey. Amy is in evening dress--her only evening dress--and over it is the cloak, which she is presently to fling back with staggering effect. Just now her pale face is hiding behind the collar of it, for she is quaking inwardly though strung up to a terrible ordeal. The room is not as she expected, but she knows that men are cunning.

AMY, frowning, 'Are these Mr. Rollo's chambers? The woman told me to knock at this door.'

She remembers with a certain satisfaction that the woman had looked at her suspiciously.

RICHARDSON, the tray in her hand to give her confidence, 'Yes, ma'am. He will be down in a minute, ma'am. He is expecting you, ma'am.'

Expecting her, is he! Amy smiles the bitter smile of knowledge.

AMY. 'We shall see.' She looks about her. Sharply, 'Where is his man?'

RICHARDSON, with the guilt of the chop on her conscience, 'What man?'

AMY, brushing this subterfuge aside, 'His man. They always have a man.'

RICHARDSON, with spirit, 'He is a man himself.'

AMY. 'Come, girl; who waits on him?'

RICHARDSON. 'Me.'

AMY, rather daunted, 'No man? Very strange.' Fortunately she sees the two plates. 'Stop.' Her eyes glisten. 'Two persons have been dining here!' Richardson begins to tremble. 'Why do you look so scared? Was the other a gentleman?'

RICHARDSON. 'Oh, ma'am.'

AMY, triumphantly, 'It was not!' But her triumph gives way to bewilderment, for she knows that when she left the house her mother was still in it. Then who can the visitor have been? 'Why are you trying to hide that plate? Was it a lady? Girl, tell me was it a lady?'

RICHARDSON, at bay, 'He--he calls her a lady.'

AMY, the omniscient, 'But you know better!'

RICHARDSON. 'Of course I know she ain't a real lady.'

AMY. 'Another woman. And not even a lady.' She has no mercy on the witness. 'Tell me, is this the first time she has dined here?'

RICHARDSON, fixed by Amy's eye, 'No, ma'am--I meant no harm, ma'am.'

AMY. 'I am not blaming *you*. Can you remember how often she has dined here?'

RICHARDSON. 'Well can I remember. Three times last week.'

AMY. 'Three times in one week, monstrous.'

RICHARDSON, with her gown to her eyes, 'Yes, ma'am; I see it now.'

AMY, considering and pouncing, 'Do you think she is an adventuress?'

RICHARDSON. 'What's that?'

AMY. 'Does she smoke cigarettes?'

RICHARDSON, rather spiritedly, 'No, she don't.'

AMY, taken aback, 'Not an adventuress.'

She wishes Ginevra were here to help her. She draws upon her stock of knowledge. 'Can she be secretly married to him? A wife of the past turned up to blackmail him? That's very common.'

RICHARDSON. 'Oh, ma'am, you are terrifying me.'

AMY. 'I wasn't talking to you. You may go. Stop. How long had she been here before I came?'

RICHARDSON. 'She--Her what you are speaking about--'

AMY. 'Come, I must know.' The terrible admission refuses to pass Richardson's lips, and of a sudden Amy has a dark suspicion. 'Has she gone! Is she here now?'

RICHARDSON. 'It was just a chop. What makes you so grudging of a chop?'

AMY. 'I don't care what they ate. Has she gone?'

RICHARDSON. 'Oh, ma'am.'

The little maid, bearing the dishes, backs to the door, opens it with her foot, and escapes from this terrible visitor. The drawn curtains attract Amy's eagle eye, and she looks behind them. There is no one there. She pulls open the door of the cupboard and says firmly, 'Come out.' No one comes. She peeps into the cupboard and finds it empty. A cupboard and no one in it. How strange. She sits down almost in tears, wishing very much for the counsel of Ginevra. Thus Steve finds her when he returns.

STEVE. 'I'm awfully glad, Alice, that you--'

He stops abruptly at sight of a strange lady. As for Amy, the word 'Alice' brings her to her feet.

AMY. 'Sir.' A short remark but withering.

STEVE. 'I beg your pardon. I thought--the fact is that I expected--You see you are a stranger to me--my name is Rollo--you are not calling on me, are you?' Amy inclines her head in a way that Ginevra and she have practised. Then she flings back her cloak as suddenly as an expert may open an umbrella. Having done this she awaits results. Steve, however, has no knowledge of how to play his part; he probably favours musical comedy. He says lamely: 'I still think there must be some mistake.'

AMY, in italics, 'There is no mistake.'

STEVE. 'Then is there anything I can do for you?'

AMY, ardently, 'You can do so much.'

STEVE. 'Perhaps if you will sit down--'

Amy decides to humour him so far. She would like to sit in the lovely stage way, when they know so precisely where the chair is that they can sit without a glance at it. But she dare not, though Ginevra would have risked it. Steve is emboldened to say: 'By the way, you have not told me *your* name.'

AMY, nervously, 'If you please, do you mind my not telling it?'

STEVE. 'Oh, very well.' First he thinks there is something innocent about her request, and then he wonders if 'innocent' is the right word. 'Well, your business, please?' he demands, like the man of the world he hopes some day to be.

AMY. 'Why are you not in evening dress?'

STEVE, taken aback, 'Does that matter?'

AMY, though it still worries her, 'I suppose not.'

STEVE, with growing stiffness, 'Your business, if you will be so good.'

Amy advances upon him. She has been seated in any case as long as they ever do sit on the stage on the same chair.

AMY. 'Stephen Rollo, the game is up.'

She likes this; she will be able to go on now.

STEVE, recoiling guiltily or so she will describe it to Ginevra, 'What on earth--'

AMY, suffering from a determination from the mouth of phrases she has collected in five theatres, 'A chance discovery, Mr. Stephen Rollo, has betrayed your secret to me.'

STEVE, awed, 'My secret? What is it?' He rushes rapidly through a well-spent youth.

AMY, risking a good deal, 'It is this: that woman is your wife.'

STEVE. 'What woman?'

AMY. 'The woman who dined with you here this evening.'

STEVE. 'With me?'

AMY, icily, 'This is useless; as I have already said, the game is up.'

STEVE, glancing in a mirror to make sure he is still the same person, 'You *look* a nice girl but dash it all. Whom can you be taking me for? Tell me some more about myself.'

AMY. Please desist. I know everything, and in a way I am sorry for you. All these years you have kept the marriage a secret, for she is a horrid sort of woman, and now she has come back to blackmail you. That, however, is not my affair.'

STEVE, with unexpected power of irony, 'Oh, I wouldn't say that.'

AMY. 'I do say it, Mr. Stephen Rollo. I shall keep your secret--'

STEVE. 'Ought you?'

AMY. '--on one condition, and on one condition only, that you return me the letters.'

STEVE. 'The letters?'

AMY. 'The letters.'

Steve walks the length of his room, regarding her sideways.

STEVE. 'Look here, honestly I don't know what you are talking about. You know, I could be angry with you, but I feel sure you are sincere.'

AMY. 'Indeed I am.'

STEVE. 'Well, then, I assure you on my word of honour that no lady was dining with me this evening, and that I have no wife.'

AMY, blankly, 'No wife! You are sure? Oh, think.'

STEVE. 'I swear it.'

AMY. 'I am very sorry.' She sinks dispiritedly into a chair.

STEVE. 'Sorry I have no wife?' She nods through her tears. 'Don't cry. How could my having a wife be a boon to you?'

AMY, plaintively, 'It would have put you in the hollow of my hands.'

STEVE, idiotically, 'And they are nice hands, too.'

AMY, with a consciousness that he might once upon a time have been saved by a good woman, 'I suppose that is how you got round her.'

STEVE, stamping his foot, 'Haven't I told you that she doesn't exist?'

AMY. 'I don't mean her--I mean her--'

He decides that she is a little crazy.

STEVE, soothingly, 'Come now, we won't go into that again. It was just a mistake; and now that it is all settled and done with, I'll tell you what we shall do. You will let me get you a cab--' She shakes her head. 'I promise not to listen to the address; and after you have had a good night you--you will see things differently.'

AMY, ashamed of her momentary weakness, and deciding not to enter it in the diary, 'You are very clever, Mr. Stephen Rollo, but I don't leave this house without the letters.'

STEVE, groaning, 'Are they your letters?'

AMY. 'How dare you! They are the letters written to you, as you well know, by--'

STEVE, eagerly, 'Yes?'

AMY. '--by a certain lady. Spare me the pain, if you are a gentleman, of having to mention her name.'

STEVE, sulkily, 'Oh, all right.'

AMY. 'She is to pass out of your life to-night. To-morrow you go abroad for a long time.'

STEVE, with excusable warmth, 'Oh, do I! Where am I going?'

AMY. 'We thought--'

STEVE. 'We?'

AMY. 'A friend and I who have been talking it over. We thought of Africa--to shoot big game.'

STEVE, humouring her, 'You must be very fond of this

lady.'

AMY. 'I would die for her.'

STEVE, feeling that he ought really to stick up a little for himself, 'After all, am I so dreadful? Why shouldn't she love me?'

AMY. 'A married woman!'

STEVE, gratified, 'Married?'

AMY. 'How can you play with me so, sir? She is my mother.'

STEVE. 'Your mother? Fond of me!'

AMY. 'How dare you look pleased.'

STEVE. 'I'm not--I didn't mean to. I say, I wish you would tell me who you are.'

AMY. 'As if you didn't know.'

STEVE, in a dream, 'Fond of me! I can't believe it.' Rather wistfully: 'How could she be?'

AMY. 'It was all your fault. Such men as you--pitiless men-- you made her love you.'

STEVE, still elated, 'Do you think I am that kind of man?'

AMY. 'Oh, sir, let her go. You are strong and she is weak. Think of her poor husband, and give me back the letters.'

STEVE. 'On my word of honour--' Here arrives Richardson, so anxious to come that she is propelled into the room like a ball. 'What is it?'

RICHARDSON. 'A gentleman downstairs, sir, wanting to see you.'

AMY, saying the right thing at once, 'He must not find me here. My reputation--'

STEVE. 'I can guess who it is. Let me think.' He is really glad of the interruption. 'See here, I'll keep him downstairs for a moment. Richardson, take this lady to the upper landing until I have brought him in. Then show her out.'

RICHARDSON. 'Oh, lor'.'

AMY, rooting herself to the floor, 'The letters!'

STEVE, as he goes, 'Write to me, write to me. I must know more of this.'

RICHARDSON. 'Come quick, Miss.'

AMY, fixing her, 'You are not deceiving me? You are sure it isn't a lady?'

RICHARDSON. 'Yes, Miss--he said his name was Colonel Grey.'

Ginevra would have known that it must be the husband, but for the moment Amy is appalled.

AMY, quivering, 'Can he suspect!'

RICHARDSON, who has her own troubles, 'About the chop?'

AMY. 'If she should come while he is here!'

RICHARDSON. 'Come along, Miss. What's the matter?'

AMY. 'I can't go away. I am not going.'

She darts into the cupboard. It is as if she had heard Ginevra cry, 'Amy, the cupboard.'

RICHARDSON, tugging at the closed door, 'Come out of that. I promised to put you on the upper landing. You can't go hiding in there, lady.'

AMY, peeping out, 'I can and I will. Let go the door. I came here expecting to have to hide.'

She closes the door as her father enters with Steve. The Colonel is chatting, but his host sees that Richardson is in distress.

STEVE, who thinks that the lady has been got rid of, 'What is it?'

RICHARDSON. 'Would you speak with me a minute, sir?'

STEVE, pointedly, 'Go away. You have some work to do on the stair. Go and do it. I'm sorry, Colonel, that you didn't bring Alice with you.'

COLONEL. 'She is coming on later.'

STEVE. 'Good.'

COLONEL. 'I have come from Pall Mall. Wanted to look in at the club once more, so I had a chop there.'

RICHARDSON, with the old sinking, 'A chop!' She departs with her worst suspicions confirmed.

STEVE, as they pull their chairs nearer to the fire, 'Is Alice coming on from home?'

COLONEL. 'Yes, that's it.' He stretches out his legs. 'Steve, home is the best club in the world. Such jolly fellows all the members!'

STEVE. 'You haven't come here to talk about your confounded baby again, have you?'

COLONEL, apologetically, 'If you don't mind.'

STEVE. 'I do mind.'

COLONEL. 'But if you feel you can stand it.'

STEVE. 'You are my guest, so go ahead.'

COLONEL. 'She fell asleep, Steve, holding my finger.'

STEVE. 'Which finger?'

COLONEL. 'This one. As Alice would say, Soldiering done, baby begun.'

STEVE. 'Poor old chap.'

COLONEL. 'I have been through a good deal in my time, Steve, but that is the biggest thing I have ever done.'

STEVE. 'Have a cigar?'

COLONEL. 'Brute! Thanks.'

Here Amy, who cannot hear when the door is closed, opens it slightly. The Colonel is presently aware that Steve is silently smiling to himself. The Colonel makes a happy guess. 'Thinking of the ladies, Steve?'

STEVE, blandly, 'To tell the truth, I *was* thinking of one.'

COLONEL. 'She seems to be a nice girl.'

STEVE. 'She is not exactly a girl.'

COLONEL, twinkling, 'Very fond of you, Steve?'

STEVE. 'I have the best of reasons for knowing that she is.' We may conceive Amy's feelings though we cannot see her. 'On my soul, Colonel, I think it is the most romantic affair I ever heard of. I have waited long for a romance to come into my life, but by Javers, it has come at last.'

COLONEL. 'Graters, Steve. Does her family like it?'

STEVE, cheerily, 'No, they are furious.'

COLONEL. 'But why?'

STEVE, judiciously, 'A woman's secret, Colonel.'

COLONEL. 'Ah, the plot thickens. Do I know her?'

STEVE. 'Not you.'

COLONEL. 'I mustn't ask her name?'

STEVE, with presence of mind, 'I have a very good reason for not telling you her name.'

COLONEL. 'So? And she is not exactly young? Twice your age, Steve?'

STEVE, with excusable heat, 'Not at all. But she is of the age when a woman knows her own mind--which makes the whole affair extraordinarily flattering.' With undoubtedly a shudder of disgust Amy closes the cupboard door. Steve continues to behave in the most gallant manner. 'You must not quiz me, Colonel, for her circumstances are such that her partiality for me puts her in a dangerous position, and I would go to the stake rather than give her away.'

COLONEL. 'Quite so.' He makes obeisance to the beauty of the sentiment, and then proceeds to an examination of the hearth-rug.

STEVE. 'What are you doing?'

COLONEL. 'Trying to find out for myself whether she comes here.'

STEVE. 'How can you find that out by crawling about my carpet?'

COLONEL. 'I am looking for hair-pins--triumphantly holding up a lady's glove--'and I have found one!'

They have been too engrossed to hear the bell ring, but now voices are audible.

STEVE. 'There is some one coming up.'

COLONEL. 'Perhaps it is *she*, Steve! No, that is Alice's voice. Catch, you scoundrel,' and he tosses him the glove. Alice is shown in, and is warmly acclaimed. She would not feel so much at ease if she knew who, hand on heart, has recognised her through the pantry key-hole.

STEVE, as he makes Alice comfortable by the fire, 'How did you leave them at home?'

ALICE, relapsing into gloom, 'All hating me.'

STEVE. 'This man says that home is the most delightful club in the world.'

ALICE. 'I am not a member; I have been blackballed by my own baby. Robert, I dined in state with Cosmo, and he was so sulky that he ate his fish without salt rather than ask me to pass it.'

COLONEL. 'Where was Amy?'

ALICE. 'Amy said she had a headache and went to bed. I spoke to her through the door before I came out, but she wouldn't answer.'

COLONEL. 'Why didn't you go in, memsahib?'

ALICE. 'I did venture to think of it, but she had locked the door. Robert, I really am worried about Amy. She seems to me to behave oddly. There can't be anything wrong?'

COLONEL. 'Of course not, Alice--eh, Steve?'

STEVE. 'Bless you, no.'

ALICE, smiling, 'It's much Steve knows about women.'

STEVE. 'I'm not so unattractive to women, Alice, as you think.'

ALICE. 'Listen to him, Robert!'

COLONEL. 'What he means, my dear, is that you should see him with elderly ladies.'

ALICE. 'Steve, this to people who know you.' Here something happens to Amy's skirt. She has opened the door to hear, then in alarm shut it, leaving a fragment of skirt caught in the door. There, unseen, it bides its time.

STEVE, darkly, 'Don't be so sure you know me, Alice.'

COLONEL, enjoying himself, 'Let us tell her, Steve! I am dying to tell her.'

STEVE, grandly, 'No, no.'

COLONEL. 'We mustn't tell you, Alice, because it is a woman's secret--a poor little fond elderly woman. Our friend is very proud of his conquest. See how he is ruffling his feathers. I shouldn't wonder you know, though you and I are in the way to-night.'

But Alice's attention is directed in another direction: to a little white object struggling in the clutches of a closed door at the back of the room. Steve turns to see what she is looking at, and at the same moment the door opens sufficiently to allow a pretty hand to obtrude, seize the kitten, or whatever it was, and softly reclose the door. For one second Alice did think it might be a kitten, but she knows now that it is part of a woman's dress. As for Steve thus suddenly acquainted with his recent visitor's whereabouts, his mouth opens wider than the door. He appeals mutely to Alice not to betray his strange secret to the Colonel.

ALICE, with dancing eyes, 'May I look about me, Steve? I have been neglecting your room shamefully.'

STEVE, alarmed, for he knows the woman, 'Don't get up, Alice; there is really nothing to see.' But she is already making the journey of the room, and drawing nearer to the door.

ALICE, playing with him, 'I like your clock.'

STEVE. 'It is my landlady's. Nearly all the things are hers. Do come back to the fire.'

ALICE. 'Don't mind me. What does this door lead into?'

STEVE. 'Only a cupboard.'

ALICE. 'What do you keep in it?'

STEVE. 'Merely crockery--that sort of thing.'

ALICE. 'I should like to see your crockery, Steve. Not one little bit of china? May I peep in?'

COLONEL, who is placidly smoking, with his back to the scene of the drama, 'Don't mind her, Steve; she never could see a door without itching to open it.'

Alice opens the door, and sees Amy standing there with her

finger to her lips, just as they stood in all the five plays. Ginevra could not have posed her better.

'Well, have you found anything, memsahib?'

It has been the great shock of Alice's life, and she sways. But she shuts the door before answering him.

ALICE, with a terrible look at Steve, 'Just a dark little cupboard.'

Steve, not aware that it is her daughter who is in there, wonders why the lighter aspect of the incident has ceased so suddenly to strike her. She returns to the fire, but not to her chair. She puts her arms round the neck of her husband; a great grief for him is welling up in her breast.

COLONEL, so long used to her dear impulsive ways, 'Hullo! We mustn't let on that we are fond of each other before company.'

STEVE, meaning well, though he had better have held his tongue, 'I don't count; I am such an old friend.'

ALICE, slowly, 'Such an old friend!' Her husband sees that she is struggling with some emotion.

COLONEL. 'Worrying about the children still, Alice?'

ALICE, glad to break down openly, 'Yes, yes, I can't help it, Robert.'

COLONEL, petting her, 'There, there, you foolish woman. Joy will come in the morning; I never was surer of anything. Would you like me to take you home now?'

ALICE. 'Home. But, yes, I--let us go home.'

COLONEL. 'Can we have a cab, Steve?'

STEVE. 'I'll go down and whistle one. Alice, I'm awfully sorry that you--that I--'

ALICE. 'Please, a cab.'

But though she is alone with her husband now she does not know what she wants to say to him. She has a passionate desire that he should not learn who is behind that door.

COLONEL, pulling her toward him, 'I think it is about Amy that you worry most.'

ALICE. 'Why should I, Robert?'

COLONEL. 'Not a jot of reason.'

ALICE. 'Say again, Robert, that everything is sure to come right just as we planned it would.'

COLONEL. 'Of course it will.'

ALICE. 'Robert, there is something I want to tell you. You know how dear my children are to me, but Amy is the dearest of all. She is dearer to me, Robert, than you yourself.'

COLONEL. 'Very well, memsahib.'

ALICE. 'Robert dear, Amy has come to a time in her life when she is neither quite a girl nor quite a woman. There are dark places before us at that age through which we have to pick our way without much help. I can conceive dead mothers haunting those places to watch how their child is to fare in them. Very frightened ghosts, Robert. I have thought so long of how I was to be within hail of my girl at this time, holding her hand--my Amy, my child.'

COLONEL. 'That is just how it is all to turn out, my Alice.'

ALICE, shivering, 'Yes, isn't it, isn't it?'

COLONEL. 'You dear excitable, of course it is.'

ALICE, like one defying him, 'But even though it were not, though I had come back too late, though my daughter had become a woman without a mother's guidance, though she were a bad woman--'

COLONEL. 'Alice.'

ALICE. 'Though some cur of a man--Robert, it wouldn't affect my love for her, I should love her more than ever. If all others turned from her, if you turned from her, Robert--how I should love her then.'

COLONEL. 'Alice, don't talk of such things.'

But she continues to talk of them, for she sees that the door is ajar, and what she says now is really to comfort Amy. Every word of it is a kiss for Amy.

ALICE, smiling through her fears, 'I was only telling you that nothing could make any difference in my love for Amy. That was all; and, of course, if she has ever been a little foolish, light-headed--at that age one often is--why, a mother would soon put all that right; she would just take her girl in her arms and they would talk it over, and the poor child's troubles would vanish.' Still for Amy's comfort, 'And do you think I should repeat any of Amy's confidences to you, Robert?' Gaily, 'Not a word, sir! She might be sure of that.'

COLONEL. 'A pretty way to treat a father. But you will never persuade me that there is any serious flaw in Amy.'

ALICE. 'I'll never try, dear.'

COLONEL. 'As for this little tantrum of locking herself into her room, however, we must have it out with her.'

ALICE. 'The first thing to-morrow.'

COLONEL. 'Not a bit of it. The first thing the moment we get home.'

ALICE, now up against a new danger, 'You forget, dear, that she has gone to bed.'

COLONEL. 'We'll soon rout her out of bed.'

ALICE. 'Robert! You forget that she has locked the door.'

COLONEL. 'Sulky little darling. I daresay she is crying her eyes out for you already. But if she doesn't open that door pretty smartly I'll force it.'

ALICE. 'You wouldn't do that?'

COLONEL. 'Wouldn't I? Oh yes, I would.'

Thus Alice has another problem to meet when Steve returns from his successful quest for a cab.

'Thank you, Steve, you will excuse us running off, I know. Alice is all nerves to-night. Come along, dear.'

ALICE, signing to the puzzled Steve that he must somehow get the lady out of the house at once, 'There is no such dreadful hurry, is there?' She is suddenly interested in some photographs on the wall. 'Are you in this group, Steve?'

STEVE. 'Yes, it is an old school eleven.'

ALICE. 'Let us see if we can pick Steve out, Robert.'

COLONEL. 'Here he is, the one with the ball.'

ALICE. 'Oh no, that can't be Steve, surely. Isn't this one more like him? Come over here under the light.'

Steve has his moment at the door, but it is evident from his face that the hidden one scorns his blandishments. So he signs to Alice.

COLONEL. 'This is you, isn't it, Steve?'

STEVE. 'Yes, the one with the ball.'

COLONEL. 'I found you at once. Now, Alice, your cloak.'

ALICE. 'I feel so comfy where I am. One does hate to leave a fire, doesn't one.' She hums gaily a snatch of a song.

COLONEL. 'The woman doesn't know her own mind.'

ALICE. 'You remember we danced to that once on my birthday at Simla.'

She shows him how they danced at Simla.

COLONEL, to Steve, who is indeed the more bewildered of the two, 'And a few minutes ago I assure you she was weeping on my shoulder!'

ALICE. 'You were so nice to me that evening, Robert--I gave you a dance.' She whirls him gaily round.

COLONEL. 'You flibberty jibbet, you make me dizzy.'

ALICE. 'Shall we sit out the rest of the dance?'

COLONEL. 'Not I. Come along, you unreasonable thing.'

ALICE. 'Unreasonable. Robert, I have a reason. I want to see whether Amy will come.'

COLONEL. 'Come?'

STEVE. 'Come here?'

ALICE. 'I didn't tell you before, Robert, because I had so little hope; but I called to her through the door that I was coming here to meet you, and I said, "I don't believe you have a headache, Amy; I believe you have locked yourself in there because you hate the poor mother who loves you," and I begged her to come with me. I said, "If you won't come now, come after me and make me happy."'

COLONEL. 'But what an odd message, Alice; so unlike you.'

ALICE. 'Was it? I don't know. I always find it so hard, Robert, to be like myself.'

COLONEL. 'But, my dear, a young girl.'

ALICE. 'She could have taken a cab; I gave her the address. Don't be so hard, Robert, I am teaching you to dance.' She is off with him again.

COLONEL. 'Steve, the madcap.'

He falls into a chair, but sees the room still going round. It is Alice's chance; she pounces upon Amy's hand, whirls her out of the hiding place, and seems to greet her at the other door.

ALICE. 'Amy!'

COLONEL, jumping up, 'Not really? Hallo! I never for a moment--It was true, then. Amy, you are a good little girl to come.'

AMY, to whom this is a not unexpected step in the game, 'Dear father.'

STEVE, to whom it is a very unexpected step indeed, 'Amy! Is this--your daughter, Alice?'

ALICE, wondering at the perfidy of the creature, 'I forgot that you don't know her, Steve.'

STEVE. 'But if--if this is your daughter--you are the mother.'

ALICE. 'The mother?'

COLONEL, jovially, 'Well thought out, Steve. He is a master mind, Alice.'

STEVE. 'But--but----'

Mercifully Amy has not lost her head. She is here to save them all.

AMY. 'Introduce me, father.'

COLONEL. 'He is astounded at our having such a big girl.'

STEVE, thankfully, 'Yes, that's it.'

COLONEL. 'Amy, my old friend, Steve Rollo--Steve, this is our rosebud.'

STEVE, blinking, 'How do you do?'

AMY, sternly, 'How do you do?'

COLONEL. 'But, bless me, Amy, you are a swell.'

AMY, flushing, 'It is only evening dress.'

COLONEL. 'I bet she didn't dress for us, Alice; it was all done for Steve.'

ALICE. 'Yes, for Steve.'

COLONEL. 'But don't hang in me, chicken, hang in your mother. Steve, why are you staring at Alice?'

We know why he is staring at Alice, but of course he is too gallant a gentleman to tell. Besides his astonishment has dazed him.

STEVE. 'Was I?'

ALICE, with her arms extended, 'Amy, don't be afraid of me.'

AMY, going into them contemptuously, 'I'm not.'

COLONEL, badgered, 'Then kiss and make it up.'

Amy bestows a cold kiss upon her mother. Alice weeps. 'This is too much. Just wait till I get you home. Are you both ready?'

It is then that Amy makes her first mistake. The glove that the Colonel has tossed to Steve is lying on a chair, and she innocently begins to put it on. Her father stares at her; his wife does not know why.

ALICE. 'We are ready, Robert. Why don't you come? Robert, what is it?'

COLONEL, darkening, 'Steve knows what it is; Amy doesn't as yet. The simple soul has given herself away so innocently that it is almost a shame to take notice of it. But I must, Steve. Come, man, it can't be difficult to explain.'

In this Steve evidently differs from him.

ALICE. 'Robert, you frighten me.'

COLONEL. 'Still tongue-tied, Steve. Before you came here,

Alice, I found a lady's glove on the floor.'

ALICE, quickly, 'That isn't our affair, Robert.'

COLONEL. 'Yes; I'll tell you why. Amy has just put on that glove.'

ALICE. 'It isn't hers, dear.'

COLONEL. 'Do you deny that it is yours, Amy?' Amy has no answer to this. 'Is it unreasonable, Steve, to ask you when my daughter, with whom you profess to be unacquainted, gave you that token of her esteem?'

STEVE, helpless, 'Alice.'

COLONEL. 'What has Alice to do with it?'

AMY, to the rescue, 'Nothing, nothing, I swear.'

COLONEL. 'Has there been something going on that I don't understand? Are you in it, Alice, as well as they? Why has Steve been staring at you so?'

AMY, knowing so well that she alone can put this matter right, 'Mother, don't answer.'

STEVE. 'If I could see Alice alone for a moment, Colonel--'

ALICE. 'Yes.'

COLONEL. 'No. Good heavens, what are you all concealing? Is Amy--my Amy--your elderly lady, Steve? Was that some tasteful little joke you were playing on your old friend, her father?'

STEVE. 'Colonel, I--'

AMY, preparing for the great sacrifice, 'I forbid him to speak.'

COLONEL. '*You* forbid him.'

ALICE. 'Robert, Robert, let me explain. Steve--'

AMY. 'Mother, you must not, you dare not.'

Grandly, 'Let all fall on me. It is not true, father, that Mr.

Rollo and I were strangers when you introduced us.'

ALICE, wailing, 'Amy, Amy.'

AMY, with a touch of the sublime, 'It *is* my glove, but it had a right to be here. He is my affianced husband.'

Perhaps, but it is an open question, Steve is the one who is most surprised to hear this. He seems to want to say something on the subject, but a look of entreaty from Alice silences him.

COLONEL. 'Alice, did you hear her?'

ALICE. 'Surely you don't mean, Robert, that you are not glad?'

COLONEL, incredulous, 'Is that how *you* take it?'

ALICE, heart-broken, 'How I take it! I am overjoyed. Don't you see how splendid it is; our old friend Steve.'

COLONEL, glaring at him, 'Our old friend, Steve.'

As for Amy, that pale-faced lily, for the moment she stands disregarded. Never mind; Ginevra will yet do her justice.

ALICE. 'Oh, happy day!' Brazenly she takes Steve's two hands, 'Robert, he is to be our son.'

COLONEL. 'You are very clever, Alice, but do you really think I believe that this is no shock to you? Oh, woman, why has this deception not struck you to the ground?'

ALICE. 'Deception? Amy, Steve, I do believe he thinks that this is as much a surprise to me as it is to him! Why, Robert, I have known about it ever since I saw Amy alone this afternoon. She told me at once. Then in came Steve, and he--'

COLONEL. 'Is it as bad as that!'

ALICE. 'As what, dear?'

COLONEL. 'That my wife must lie to me.'

ALICE. 'Oh, Robert.'

COLONEL. 'I am groping only, but I can see now that you felt there was something wrong from the first. How did you find out?'

ALICE, imploringly, 'Robert, they are engaged to be married; it was foolish of them not to tell you; but, oh, my dear, leave it at that.'

COLONEL. 'Why did you ask Amy to follow us here?'

ALICE. 'So that we could all be together when we broke it to you, dear.'

COLONEL. 'Another lie! My shoulders are broad; why shouldn't I have it to bear as well as you?'

ALICE. 'There is nothing to bear but just a little folly.'

COLONEL. 'Folly! And neither of them able to say a word?'

Indeed they are very cold lovers; Amy's lip is curled at Steve. To make matters worse, the cupboard door, which has so far had the decency to remain quiet, now presumes to have its say. It opens of itself a few inches, creaking guiltily. Three people are so startled that a new suspicion is roused in the fourth.

ALICE, who can read his face so well, 'She wasn't there, Robert, she wasn't.'

COLONEL. 'My God! I understand now; she didn't follow us; she hid there when I came.'

ALICE. 'No, Robert, no.'

He goes into the cupboard and returns with something in his hand, which he gives to Amy.

COLONEL. 'Your other glove, Amy.'

ALICE. 'I can't keep it from you any longer, Robert; I have done my best.' She goes to Amy to protect her. 'But Amy is still my child.'

'What a deceiver' Amy is thinking.

COLONEL. 'Well, sir, still waiting for that interview with my wife before you can say anything?'

STEVE, a desperate fellow, 'Yes.'

ALICE. 'You will have every opportunity of explaining, Steve, many opportunities; but in the meantime--just now, please go, leave us alone.' Stamping her foot: 'Go, please.'

Steve has had such an evening of it that he clings dizzily to the one amazing explanation, that Alice loves him not wisely but too well. Never will he betray her, never.

STEVE, with a meaning that is lost on her but is very evident to the other lady present,

'Anything *you* ask me to do, Alice, anything. I shall go up-stairs only, so that if you want me--'

ALICE. 'Oh, go.' He goes, wondering whether he is a villain or a hero, which is perhaps a pleasurable state of mind.

COLONEL. 'You are wondrous lenient to him; I shall have more to say. As for this girl--look at her standing there, she seems rather proud of herself.'

ALICE. 'It isn't really hardness, Robert. It is because she thinks that you are hard. Robert, dear, I want you to go away too, and leave Amy to me. Go home, Robert; we shall follow soon.'

COLONEL, after a long pause, 'If you wish it.'

ALICE. 'Leave her to her mother.'

When he has gone Amy leans across the top of a chair, sobbing her little heart away. Alice tries to take her--the whole of her--in her arms, but is rebuffed with a shudder.

AMY. 'I wonder you can touch me.'

ALICE. 'The more you ask of your mother the more she has

to give. It is my love you need, Amy; and you can draw upon it, and draw upon it.'

AMY. 'Pray excuse me.'

ALICE. 'How can you be so hard! My child, I am not saying one harsh word to you. I am asking you only to hide your head upon your mother's breast.'

AMY. 'I decline.'

ALICE. 'Take care, Amy, or I shall begin to believe that your father was right. What do you think would happen if I were to leave you to him!'

AMY. 'Poor father.'

ALICE. 'Poor indeed with such a daughter.'

AMY. 'He has gone, mother; so do you really think you need keep up this pretence before me?'

ALICE. 'Amy, what you need is a whipping.'

AMY. 'You ought to know what I need.'

The agonised mother again tries to envelop her unnatural child.

ALICE. 'Amy, Amy, it was all Steve's fault.'

AMY, struggling as with a boa constrictor, 'You needn't expect me to believe that.'

ALICE. 'No doubt you thought at the beginning that he was a gallant gentleman.'

AMY. 'Not at all; I knew he was depraved from the moment I set eyes on him.'

ALICE. 'My Amy! Then how--how--'

AMY. 'Ginevra knew too.'

ALICE. 'She knew!'

AMY. 'We planned it together--to treat him in the same way

as Sir Harry Paskill and Ralph Devereux.'

ALICE. 'Amy, you are not in your senses. You don't mean that there were others?'

AMY. 'There was Major--Major--I forget his name, but he was another.'

ALICE, shaking her, 'Wretched girl.'

AMY. 'Leave go.'

ALICE. 'How did you get to know them?'

AMY. 'To know them? They are characters in plays.'

ALICE, bereft, 'Characters in plays? Plays!'

AMY. 'We went to five last week.'

Wild hopes spring up in Alice's breast.

ALICE. 'Amy, tell me quickly, when did you see Steve for the first time?'

AMY. 'When you were saying good-bye to him this afternoon.'

ALICE. 'Can it be true!'

AMY. 'Perhaps we shouldn't have listened; but they always listen when there is a screen.'

ALICE. 'Listened? What did you hear?'

AMY. 'Everything, mother! We saw him kiss you and heard you make an assignation to meet him here.'

ALICE. 'I shall whip you directly, but go on, darling.'

AMY, childishly, 'You shan't whip me.' Then once more heroic, 'As in a flash Ginevra and I saw that there was only one way to save you. I must go to his chambers, and force him to return the letters.'

ALICE, inspired, 'My letters?'

AMY. 'Of course. He behaved at first as they all do--pretended that he did not know what I was talking about. At that moment, a visitor; I knew at once that it must be the husband; it always is, it was; I hid. Again a visitor. I knew it must be you, it was; oh, the agony to me in there. I was wondering when he would begin to suspect, for I knew the time would come, and I stood ready to emerge and sacrifice myself to save you.'

ALICE. 'As you have done, Amy?'

AMY. 'As I have done.'

Once more the arms go round her.

'I want none of that.'

ALICE. 'Forgive me.' A thought comes to Alice that enthralls her. 'Steve! Does he know what you think--about me?'

AMY. 'I had to be open with him.'

ALICE. 'And Steve believes it? He thinks that I--I--Alice Grey--oh, ecstasy!'

AMY. 'You need not pretend.'

ALICE. 'What is to be done?'

AMY. 'Though I abhor him I must marry him for aye. Ginevra is to be my only bridesmaid. We are both to wear black.'

ALICE, sharply, 'You are sure you don't rather like him, Amy?'

AMY. 'Mother!'

ALICE. 'Amy, weren't you terrified to come alone to the rooms of a man you didn't even know? Some men--'

AMY. 'I was not afraid. I am a soldier's daughter; and Ginevra gave me this.'

She produces a tiny dagger. This is altogether too much for Alice.

ALICE. 'My darling!'

She does have the babe in her arms at last, and now Amy clings to her. This is very sweet to Alice; but she knows that if she tells Amy the truth at once its first effect will be to make the dear one feel ridiculous. How can Alice hurt her Amy so, Amy who has such pride in having saved her? 'You do love me a little, Amy, don't you?'

AMY. 'Yes, yes.'

ALICE. 'You don't think I have been really bad, dear?'

AMY. 'Oh, no, only foolish.'

ALICE. 'Thank you, Amy.'

AMY, nestling still closer, 'What are we to do now, dear dear mother?'

Alice has a happy idea; but that, as the novelists say, deserves a chapter to itself.

III

We are back in the room of the diary. The diary itself is not visible; it is tucked away in the drawer, taking a nap while it may, for it has much to chronicle before cockcrow. Cosmo also is asleep, on an ingenious arrangement of chairs. Ginevra is sitting bolt upright, a book on her knee, but she is not reading it. She is seeing visions in which Amy plays a desperate part. The hour is late; every one ought to be in bed.

Cosmo is perhaps dreaming that he is back at Osborne, for he calls out, as if in answer to a summons, that he is up and nearly dressed. He then raises his head and surveys Ginevra.

COSMO. 'Hullo, you've been asleep.'

GINEVRA. 'How like a man.'

COSMO. 'I say, I thought you were the one who had stretched herself out, and that I was sitting here very quiet, so as not to waken you.'

GINEVRA. 'Let us leave it at that.'

COSMO. 'Huffy, aren't you! Have they not come back yet?'

GINEVRA. 'Not they. And half-past eleven has struck. I oughtn't to stay any longer; as it is, I don't know what my land-lady will say.'

She means that she does know.

COSMO. 'I'll see you to your place whenever you like. My uniform will make it all right for you.'

GINEVRA. 'You child. But I simply can't go till I know what has happened. Where, oh where, can they be?'

COSMO. 'That's all right. Father told you he had a message from mother saying that they had gone to the theatre.'

GINEVRA. 'But why?'

COSMO. 'Yes, it seemed to bother him, too.'

GINEVRA. 'The theatre. That is what she *said*.'

Here Cosmo takes up a commanding position on the hearth-rug; it could not be bettered unless with a cigar in the mouth.

COSMO. 'Look here, Miss Dunbar, it may be that I have a little crow to pick with mother when she comes back, but I can-not allow anyone else to say a word against her. Comprenez?'

Ginevra's reply is lost to the world because at this moment Amy's sparkling eyes show round the door. How softly she must have crossed the little hall!

GINEVRA. 'Amy, at last!'

AMY. 'Sh!' She speaks to some one unseen, 'There are only Ginevra and Cosmo here.'

Thus encouraged Alice enters. Despite her demeanour they would see, if they knew her better, that she has been having a good time, and is in hopes that it is not ended yet. She comes in, as it were, under Amy's guidance. Ginevra is introduced, and Alice then looks to Amy for instructions what to do next.

AMY, encouragingly, 'Sit down, mother.'

ALICE. 'Where shall I sit, dear?' Amy gives her the nicest chair in the room. 'Thank you, Amy.' She is emboldened to address her son. 'Where is your father, Cosmo?'

Cosmo remembers his slap, and that he has sworn to converse with her no more. He indicates, however, that his father is in the room overhead. Alice meekly accepts the rebuff. 'Shall I go to him, Amy?'

AMY, considerately, 'If you think you feel strong enough, mother.'

ALICE. 'You have given me strength.'

AMY. 'I am so glad.' She strokes her mother soothingly. '*What will you tell him?*'

ALICE. 'All, Amy--all, all.'

AMY. 'Brave mother.'

ALICE. 'Who could not be brave with such a daughter.' On reflection, 'And with such a son.'

Helped by encouraging words from Amy she departs on her perilous enterprise. The two conspirators would now give a handsome competence to Cosmo to get him out of the room. He knows it, and sits down.

COSMO, 'I say, what is she going to tell father?'

AMY, with a despairing glance at Ginevra, 'Oh, nothing.'

GINEVRA, with a clever glance at Amy, 'Cosmo, you promised to see me home.'

COSMO, the polite, 'Right O.'

GINEVRA. 'But you haven't got your boots on.'

COSMO. 'I won't be a minute.' He pauses at the door. 'I say I believe you're trying to get rid of me. Look here, I won't budge till you tell me what mother is speaking about to father.'

AMY. 'It is about the drawing-room curtains.'

COSMO. 'Good lord!' As soon as he has gone they rush at each other; they don't embrace; they stop when their noses are an inch apart, and then talk. This is the stage way for lovers. It is difficult to accomplish without rubbing noses, but they have both been practising.

GINEVRA. 'Quick, Amy, did you get the letters?'

AMY. 'There are no letters.'

Ginevra is so taken aback that her nose bobs. Otherwise the two are absolutely motionless. She cleverly recovers herself.

GINEVRA. 'No letters; how unlike life. You are quite sure?'

AMY. 'I have my mother's word for it.'

GINEVRA. 'Is that enough?'

AMY. 'And you now have mine.'

GINEVRA. 'Then it hadn't gone far?'

AMY. 'No, merely a painful indiscretion. But if father had known it--you know what husbands are.'

GINEVRA. 'Yes, indeed. Did he follow her?'

Amy nods. 'Did you hide?' Amy nods again.

AMY. 'Worse than that, Ginevra. To deceive him I had to pretend that I was the woman. And now--Ginevra, can you guess?--' Here they have to leave off doing noses. On the stage it can be done for ever so much longer, but only by those who are paid accordingly.

GINEVRA. 'You don't mean--?'

AMY. 'I think I do, but what do you mean?'

GINEVRA. 'I mean--the great thing.'

AMY. 'Then it is, yes. Ginevra, I am affianced to the man, Steve!' Ginevra could here quickly drink a glass of water if there was one in the room.

GINEVRA, wandering round her old friend, 'You seem the same, Amy, yet somehow different.'

AMY, rather complacently, 'That is just how I feel. But I must not think of myself. They are overhead, Ginevra. There is an awful scene taking place--up there. She is telling father all.'

GINEVRA. 'Confessing?'

AMY. 'Everything--in a noble attempt to save me from a widowed marriage.'

GINEVRA. 'But I thought she was such a hard woman.'

AMY. 'Not really. To the world perhaps; but I have softened her. All she needed, Ginevra, to bring out her finer qualities was a strong nature to lean upon; and she says that she has found it in me. At the theatre and all the way home--'

GINEVRA. 'Then you did go to the theatre. Why?'

AMY, feeling that Ginevra is very young, 'Need you ask? Oh, Ginevra, to see if we could find a happy ending. It was mother's idea.'

GINEVRA. 'Which theatre?'

AMY. 'I don't know, but the erring wife confessed all--in one of those mousselines de soie that are so fashionable this year; and mother and I sat--clasping each other's hands, praying it might end happily, though we didn't see how it could.'

GINEVRA. 'How awful for you. What did the husband do?'

AMY. 'He was very calm and white. He went out of the room

for a moment, and came back so white. Then he sat down by the fire, and nodded his head three times.'

GINEVRA. 'I think I know now which theatre it was.'

AMY. 'He asked her coldly--but always the perfect gentleman----'

GINEVRA. 'Oh, that theatre.'

AMY. 'He asked her whether *he* was to go or she.'

GINEVRA. 'They must part?'

AMY. 'Yes. She went on her knees to him, and said "Are we never to meet again?" and he replied huskily "Never." Then she turned and went slowly towards the door.'

GINEVRA, clutching her, 'Amy, was that the end?'

AMY. 'The audience sat still as death, listening for the awful *click* that brings the curtain down.'

GINEVRA, shivering, 'I seem to hear it.'

AMY. 'At that moment--'

GINEVRA. 'Yes, yes?'

AMY. 'The door opened, and, Ginevra, their little child--came in--in her night-gown.'

GINEVRA. 'Quick.'

AMY. 'She came toddling down the stairs--she was barefooted--she took in the whole situation at a glance--and, running to her father, she said, "Daddy, if mother goes away what is to become of me?"' Amy gulps and continues: 'And then she took a hand of each and drew them together till they fell on each other's breasts, and then--Oh, Ginevra, then--Click!--and the curtain fell.'

GINEVRA, when they are more composed, 'How old was the child?'

AMY. 'Five. She looked more.'

GINEVRA, her brows knitted, 'Molly is under two, isn't she?'

AMY. 'She is not quite twenty months.'

GINEVRA. 'She couldn't possibly do it.'

AMY. 'No; I thought of that. But she couldn't, you know, even though she was held up. Mother couldn't help thinking the scene was a good omen, though.' They both look at the ceiling again. 'How still they are.'

GINEVRA. 'Perhaps she hasn't had the courage to tell.'

AMY. 'If so, I must go on with it.'

GINEVRA, feeling rather small beside Amy, 'Marry him?'

AMY. 'Yes. I must dree my weird. Is it dree your weird, or weird your dree?'

GINEVRA. 'I think they both do.' She does not really care; nobler thoughts are surging within her. 'Amy, why can't I make some sacrifice as well as you?'

Amy seems about to make a somewhat grudging reply, but the unexpected arrival of the man who has so strangely won her seals her lips.

AMY. 'You!' with a depth of meaning, 'Oh, sir.'

STEVE, the most nervous of the company, 'I felt I must come. Miss Grey, I am in the greatest distress, as the unhappy cause of all this trouble.'

AMY, coldly, 'You should have thought of that before.'

STEVE. 'It was dense of me not to understand sooner--very dense.' He looks at her with wistful eyes. 'Must I marry you, Miss Grey?'

AMY, curling her lip, 'Ah, that is what you are sorry for!'

STEVE. 'Yes--horribly sorry.' Hastily, 'Not for myself. To tell you the truth, I'd be--precious glad to risk it--I think.'

AMY, with a glance at Ginevra, 'You would?'

STEVE. 'But very sorry for you. It seems such a shame to you--so young and attractive--and the little you know of me so--unfortunate.'

AMY. 'You mean you could never love me?'

STEVE. 'I don't mean that at all.'

AMY. 'Ginevra!'

Indeed Ginevra feels that she has been obliterated quite long enough.

GINEVRA, with a touch of testiness in her tone, 'Amy--introduce me.'

AMY. 'Mr. Stephen Rollo--Miss Dunbar. Miss Dunbar knows all.'

Ginevra makes a movement that the cynical might describe as brushing Amy aside.

GINEVRA. 'May I ask, Mr. Rollo, what are your views about woman?'

STEVE. 'Really I--'

GINEVRA. 'Is she, in your opinion, her husband's equal, or is she his chattel?'

STEVE. 'Honestly, I am so beside myself--'

GINEVRA. 'You evade the question.'

AMY. 'He means chattel, Ginevra.'

GINEVRA. 'Mr. Rollo, I am the friend till death of Amy Grey. Let that poor child go, sir, and I am prepared to take her place beside you--Yes, at the altar's mouth.'

AMY. 'Ginevra.'

GINEVRA, making that movement again, 'Understand I can neither love nor honour you--at least at first--but I will obey you.'

AMY. 'Ginevra, you take too much upon yourself.'

GINEVRA. 'I *will* make a sacrifice--I will.'

AMY. 'You shall not.'

GINEVRA. 'I feel that I understand this gentleman as no other woman can. It is my mission, Amy--' The return of Alice is what prevents Steve's seizing his hat and flying. It might not have had this effect had he seen the lady's face just before she opened the door.

ALICE, putting her hand to her poor heart, 'You have come here, Steve? Oh no, it is not possible.'

STEVE, looking things unutterable, 'How could I help coming?'

AMY, to the rescue, 'Mother, have you--did you?'

ALICE, meekly, 'I have told him all.'

STEVE. 'The Colonel?'

Alice bows her bruised head.

AMY, conducting her to a seat, 'Brave, brave. What has he decided?'

ALICE. 'He hasn't decided yet. He is thinking out what it will be best to do.'

STEVE. 'He knows? Then I am no longer--' His unfinished sentence seems to refer to Amy.

AMY, proudly, 'Yes, sir, as he knows, you are, as far as I am concerned, now free.'

GINEVRA, in a murmur, 'It's almost a pity.' She turns to her Amy. 'At least, Amy, this makes you and me friends again.' We have never quite been able to understand what this meant, but Amy knows, for she puts Ginevra's hand to her sweet lips.

ALICE, who somehow could do without Ginevra to-night, 'Cosmo is waiting for you, Miss Dunbar, to see you home.'

GINEVRA, with a disquieting vision of her landlady, 'I must go.' She gives her hand in the coldest way to Mrs. Grey. Then, with a curtsey to Steve that he can surely never forget, 'Mr. Rollo, I am sure there is much good in you. Darling Amy, I shall be round first thing in the morning.'

STEVE. 'Now that she has gone, can we--have a talk?'

ALICE, looking down, 'Yes, Steve.'

AMY, gently, 'Mother, what was that you called him?'

ALICE. 'Dear Amy, I forgot. Yes, Mr. Rollo.'

STEVE. 'Then, Alice--'

AMY. 'This lady's name, if I am not greatly mistaken, is Mrs. Grey. Is it not so, mother?'

ALICE. 'Yes, Amy.'

STEVE. 'As you will; but it is most important that I say certain things to her at once.'

ALICE. 'Oh, Mr. Rollo. What do you think, dear?'

AMY, reflecting, 'If it be clearly understood that this is good-bye, I consent. Please be as brief as possible.'

Somehow they think that she is moving to the door, but she crosses only to the other side of the room and sits down with a book. One of them likes this very much.

STEVE, who is not the one, 'But I want to see her alone.'

AMY, the dearest of little gaolers, 'That, I am afraid, I cannot permit. It is not that I have not perfect confidence in you, mother, but you must see I am acting wisely.'

ALICE. 'Yes, Amy.'

STEVE, to his Alice, 'What has come over you? You don't seem to be the same woman.'

AMY. 'That is just it; she is not.'

ALICE. 'I see now only through Amy's eyes.'

AMY. 'They will not fail you, mother. Proceed, sir.'

Steve has to make the best of it.

STEVE. 'You told him, then, about your feelings for me?'

ALICE, studying the carpet, 'He knows now exactly what are my feelings for you.'

STEVE, huskily, 'How did he take it?'

ALICE. 'Need you ask?'

STEVE. 'Poor old boy. I suppose he wishes me to stay away from your house now.'

ALICE. 'Is it unreasonable?'

STEVE. 'No, of course not, but--'

ALICE. 'Will it be terribly hard to you, St--Mr. Rollo?'

STEVE. 'It isn't that. You see I'm fond of the Colonel, I really am, and it hurts me to think he thinks that I--It wasn't my fault, was it?'

AMY. 'Ungenerous.'

ALICE. 'He quite understands that it was I who lost my head.'

Steve is much moved by the generosity of this. He lowers his voice.

STEVE. 'Of course I blame myself now; but I assure you honestly I had no idea of it until to-night. I had thought you were only my friend. It dazed me; but as I ransacked my mind many little things came back to me. I remembered what I hadn't noticed at the time--'

AMY. 'Louder, please.'

STEVE. 'I remembered--'

AMY. 'Is this necessary?'

ALICE. 'Please, Amy, let me know what he remembered.'

STEVE. 'I remembered that your voice was softer to me than when you were addressing other men.'

ALICE. 'Let me look long at you, Mr. Rollo.' She looks long at him.

AMY. 'Mother, enough.'

ALICE. 'What more do you remember?'

STEVE. 'It is strange to me now that I didn't understand your true meaning to-day when you said I was the only man you couldn't flirt with; you meant that I aroused deeper feelings.'

ALICE. 'How you know me.'

AMY. 'Not the best of you, mother.'

ALICE. 'No, not the best, Amy.'

STEVE. 'I can say that I never thought of myself as possessing dangerous qualities. I thought I was utterly unattractive to women.'

ALICE. 'You *must* have known about your eyes.'

STEVE, eagerly, 'My eyes? On my soul I didn't.'

Amy wonders if this can be true. Alice rises. She feels that she cannot control herself much longer.

ALICE. 'Steve, if you don't go away at once I shall scream.'

STEVE, really unhappy, 'Is it as bad as that?'

AMY, rising, 'You heard what Mrs. Grey said. This is very painful to her. Will you please say good-bye.'

In the novel circumstances he does not quite know how this

should be carried out.

ALICE, also shy, 'How shall we do it, Amy? On the brow?'

AMY. 'No, mother--with the hand.'

They do it with the hand, and it is thus that the Colonel finds them. He would be unable to keep his countenance were it not for a warning look from Alice.

COLONEL, one of the men who have a genius for saying the right thing, 'Ha.'

STEVE. 'I am going, Colonel. I am very sorry that you----At the same time I wish you to understand that the fault is entirely mine.'

COLONEL, guardedly, 'Ha.'

AMY, putting an arm round her mother, who hugs it, 'Father, he came only to say goodbye. He is not a bad man, and mother has behaved magnificently.'

COLONEL, cleverly, 'Ha.'

AMY. 'You must not, you shall not, be cruel to her.'

ALICE. 'Darling Amy.'

COLONEL, truculently, 'Oh, mustn't I. We shall see about that.'

STEVE. 'Come, come, Colonel.'

COLONEL, doing better than might have been expected, 'Hold your tongue, sir.'

AMY. 'I know mother as no other person can know her. I begin to think that you have no proper appreciation of her, father.'

ALICE, basely, 'Dear, dear Amy.'

AMY. 'I daresay she has often suffered in the past--'

ALICE. 'Oh, Amy, oh.'

AMY. 'By your--your callousness--your want of sympathy--

your neglect.'

ALICE. 'My beloved child.'

COLONEL, uneasily, 'Alice, tell her it isn't so.'

ALICE. 'You hear what he says, my pet.'

AMY. 'But you don't deny it.'

COLONEL. 'Deny it, woman.'

ALICE. 'Robert, Robert.'

AMY. 'And please not to call my mother "woman" in my presence.'

COLONEL. 'I--I--I----' He looks for help from Alice, but she gives him only a twinkle of triumph. He barks, 'Child, go to your room.'

AMY, her worst fears returning, 'But what are you going to do?'

COLONEL. 'That is not your affair.'

STEVE. 'I must say I don't see that.'

AMY, gratefully, 'Thank you, Mr. Rollo.'

COLONEL. 'Go to your room.'

She has to go, but not till she has given her mother a kiss that is a challenge to the world. Then to the bewilderment of Steve two human frames are rocked with laughter.

ALICE. 'Oh, Robert, look at him. He thinks I worship him.'

COLONEL. 'Steve, you colossal puppy.'

STEVE. 'Eh--what--why?'

ALICE. 'Steve, tell Robert about my voice being softer to you than to other men; tell him, Steve, about your eyes.'

The unhappy youth gropes mentally and physically.

STEVE. 'Good heavens, was there nothing in it?'

COLONEL. 'My boy, I'll never let you hear the end of this.'

STEVE. 'But if there's nothing in it, how could your daughter have thought--'

COLONEL. 'She saw you kiss Alice here this afternoon, you scoundrel, and, as she thought, make an *assignation* with you. There, it all came out of that. She is a sentimental lady, is our Amy, and she has been too often to the theatre.'

STEVE. 'Let me think.'

COLONEL. 'Here is a chair for the very purpose. Now, think hard.'

STEVE. 'But--but--then why did you pretend before her, Alice?'

ALICE. 'Because she thinks that she has saved me, and it makes her so happy. Amy has a passionate desire to be of some use in this world she knows so well, and she already sees her sphere, Steve, it is to look after me. I am not to be her chaperone, it is she who is to be mine. I have submitted, you see.'

COLONEL, fidgeting, 'She seems to have quite given me up for you.'

ALICE, blandly, 'Oh yes, Robert, quite.'

STEVE, gloomily, 'You will excuse my thinking only of myself. What an ass I've been.'

ALICE. 'Is it a blow, Steve?'

STEVE. 'It's a come down. Ass, ass, ass! But I say, Alice, I'm awfully glad it's I who have been the ass and not you. I really am, Colonel. You see the tragedy of my life is I'm such an extraordinarily ordinary sort of fellow that, though every man I know says some lady has loved him, there never in all my unromantic life was a woman who cared a Christmas card for me. It often makes me lonely; and so when I thought such a glorious woman as you,

Alice--I lost touch of earth altogether; but now I've fallen back on it with a whack. But I'm glad--yes, I'm glad. You two kindest people Steve Rollo has ever known.--Oh, I say good-night. I suppose you can't overlook it, Alice.'

ALICE. 'Oh, yes, you goose, I can. We are both fond of you--Mr. Rollo.'

COLONEL. 'Come in, my boy, and make love to *me* as often as you feel lonely.'

STEVE. 'I may still come to see you? I say, I'm awfully taken with your Amy.'

COLONEL. 'None of that, Steve.'

ALICE. '*We* can drop in on you on the sly, Steve, to admire your orbs; but you mustn't come here--until Amy thinks it is safe for me.' When he has gone she adds, 'Until I think it is safe for Amy.'

COLONEL. 'When will that be?'

ALICE. 'Not for some time.'

COLONEL. 'He isn't a bad sort, Steve.'

ALICE. 'Oh, no--she might even do worse some day. But she is to be my little girl for a long time first.'

COLONEL. 'This will give him a sort of glamour to her, you know.'

ALICE. 'You are not really thinking, Robert, that my Amy is to fall asleep to-night before she hears the whole true story. Could I sleep until she knows everything!'

COLONEL. 'Stupid of me. I am a little like Steve in one way, though; I don't understand why you have kept it up so long.'

ALICE. 'It isn't the first time you have thought me a harum-scarum.'

COLONEL. 'It isn't.'

ALICE. 'The sheer fun of it, Robert, went to my head, I suppose. And then, you see, the more Amy felt herself to be my protectress the more she seemed to love me. I am afraid I have a weakness for the short cuts to being loved.'

COLONEL. 'I'm afraid you have. The one thing you didn't think of is that the more she loves you the less love she seems to have for me.'

ALICE. 'How selfish of you, Robert.'

COLONEL, suspiciously, 'Or was that all part of the plan?'

ALICE. 'There was no plan; there wasn't time for one. But you were certainly rather horrid, Robert, in the way you gloated over me when you saw them take to you. I have been gloating a little perhaps in taking them from you.'

COLONEL. 'Them? You are going a little too fast, my dear. I have still got Cosmo and Molly.'

ALICE. 'For the moment.'

COLONEL. 'Woman.'

ALICE. 'Remember, Amy said you must not call me that.'

He laughs as he takes her by the shoulders.

'Yes, shake me; I deserve it.'

COLONEL. 'You do, indeed,' and he shakes her with a ferocity that would have startled any sudden visitor. No wonder, then, that it is a shock to Cosmo, who comes blundering in. Alice is the first to see him, and she turns the advantage to unprincipled account.

ALICE. 'Robert, don't hurt me. Oh, if Cosmo were to see you!'

COSMO. 'Cosmo does see him.' He says it in a terrible voice.

Probably Cosmo has been to a theatre or two himself.

ALICE. 'You here, Cosmo!'

She starts back from her assailant.

COLONEL, feeling a little foolish, 'I didn't hear you come in.'

COSMO, grimly, 'No, I'm sure you didn't.'

COLONEL, testily, 'No heroics, my boy.'

COSMO. 'Take care, father.' He stands between them, which makes his father suddenly grin. 'Laugh on, sir. I don't know what this row's about, but'--here his arm encircles an undeserving lady--'this lady is my mother, and I won't have her bullied. What's a father compared to a mother.'

ALICE. 'Cosmo, darling Cosmo.'

COLONEL, becoming alarmed, 'My boy, it was only a jest. Alice, tell him it was only a jest.'

ALICE. 'He says it was only a jest, Cosmo.'

COSMO. 'You are a trump to shield him, mother.' He kisses her openly, conscious that he is a bit of a trump himself, in which view Alice most obviously concurs.

COLONEL, to his better half, 'You serpent.'

COSMO. 'Sir, this language won't do.'

COLONEL, exasperated, 'You go to bed, too.'

ALICE. 'He has sent Amy to bed already. Try to love your father, Cosmo,' placing many kisses on the spot where he had been slapped. *Try for my sake*, and try to get Amy and Molly to do it, too.' Sweetly to her husband, 'They will love you in time, Robert; at present they can think only of me. Darling, I'll come and see you in bed.'

COSMO. 'I don't like to leave you with him--'

ALICE. 'Go, my own; I promise to call out if I need you.'

On these terms Cosmo departs. The long-suffering husband, arms folded, surveys his unworthy spouse.

COLONEL. 'You *are* a hussy.'

ALICE, meekly, 'I suppose I am.'

COLONEL. 'Mind you, I am not going to stand Cosmo's thinking this of me.'

ALICE. 'As if I would allow it for another hour! You won't see much of me to-night, Robert. If I sleep at all it will be in Amy's room.'

COLONEL, lugubriously, 'You will be taking Molly from me to-morrow.'

ALICE. 'I feel hopeful that Molly, too, will soon be taking care of me.' She goes to him in her cajoling way: 'With so many chaperones, Robert, I ought to do well. Oh, my dear, don't think that I have learnt no lesson to-night.'

COLONEL, smiling, 'Going to reform at last?'

ALICE, the most serious of women, 'Yes, Robert. The Alice you have known is come to an end. To-morrow--'

COLONEL. 'If she is different to-morrow I'll disown her.'

ALICE. 'It's summer done, autumn begun. Farewell, summer, we don't know you any more. My girl and I are like the little figures in the weather-house; when Amy comes out, Alice goes in. Alice Sit-by-the-fire henceforth. The moon is full to-night, Robert, but it isn't looking for me any more. Taxis farewell--advance four-wheelers. I had a beautiful husband once, black as the raven was his hair--'

COLONEL. 'Stop it.'

ALICE. 'Pretty Robert, farewell. Farewell, Alice that was; it's all over, my dear. I always had a weakness for you; but now you must really go; make way there for the old lady.'

COLONEL. 'Woman, you'll make me cry. Go to your Amy.'

ALICE. 'Robert--'

COLONEL. 'Go. Go. Go.'

As he roars it Amy peeps in anxiously. She is in her night-gown, and her hair is down and her feet are bare, and she does not look so very much more than five. Alice is unable to resist the temptation.

ALICE, wailing, 'Must I go, Robert?'

AMY. 'Going away? Mother! Father, if mother goes away, what is to become of me?'

She draws them together until their hands clasp. There is now a beatific smile on her face. The curtain sees that its time has come; it clicks, and falls.

THE END

www.bookjungle.com *email: sales@bookjungle.com fax: 630-214-0564 mail: Book Jungle PO Box 2226 Champaign, IL 61825*

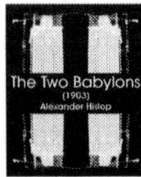

The Two Babylons
Alexander Hislop   QTY

You may be surprised to learn that many traditions of Roman Catholicism in fact don't come from Christ's teachings but from an ancient Babylonian "Mystery" religion that was centered on Nimrod, his wife Semiramis, and a child Tammuz. This book shows how this ancient religion transformed itself as it incorporated Christ into its teachings....

Religion/History   Pages:358

ISBN: *1-59462-010-5*   *MSRP* **$22.95**

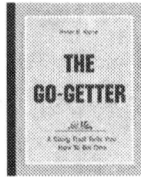

The Go-Getter
Kyne B. Peter   QTY

The Go Getter is the story of William Peck.He was a war veteran and amputee who will not be refused what he wants. Peck not only fights to find employment but continually proves himself more than competent at the many difficult test that are throw his way in the course of his early days with the Ricks Lumber Company...

Business/Self Help/Inspirational   Pages:68

ISBN: *1-59462-186-1*   *MSRP* **$8.95**

The Power Of Concentration
Theron Q. Dumont

It is of the utmost value to learn how to concentrate. To make the greatest success of anything you must be able to concentrate your entire thought upon the idea you are working on. The person that is able to concentrate utilizes all constructive thoughts and shuts out all destructive ones...

Self Help/Inspirational   Pages:196

ISBN: *1-59462-141-1*   *MSRP* **$14.95**

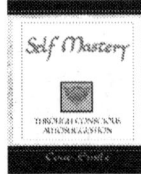

Self Mastery
Emile Coue

Emile Coue came up with novel way to improve the lives of people. He was a pharmacist by trade and often saw ailing people. This lead him to develop autosuggestion, a form of self-hypnosis. At the time his theories weren't popular but over the years evidence is mounting that he was indeed right all along...

New Age/Self Help   Pages:98

ISBN: *1-59462-189-6*   *MSRP* **$7.95**

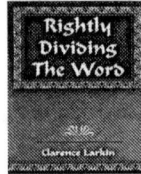

Rightly Dividing The Word
Clarence Larkin

The "Fundamental Doctrines" of the Christian Faith are clearly outlined in numerous books on Theology, but they are not available to the average reader and were mainly written for students. The Author has made it the work of his ministry to preach the "Fundamental Doctrines." To this end he has aimed to express them in the simplest and clearest manner..

Religion   Pages:352

ISBN: *1-59462-334-1*   *MSRP* **$23.45**

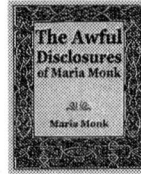

The Awful Disclosures Of
Maria Monk

"I cannot banish the scenes and characters of this book from my memory. To me it can never appear like an amusing fable, or lose its interest and importance. The story is one which is continually before me, and must return fresh to my mind with painful emotions as long as I live..."

Religion   Pages:232

ISBN: *1-59462-160-8*   *MSRP* **$17.95**

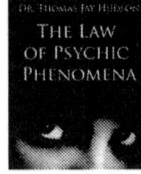

The Law of Psychic Phenomena
Thomson Jay Hudson

"I do not expect this book to stand upon its literary merits; for if it is unsound in principle, felicity of diction cannot save it, and if sound, homeliness of expression cannot destroy it. My primary object in offering it to the public is to assist in bringing Psychology within the domain of the exact sciences. That this has never been accomplished..."

New Age   Pages:420

ISBN: *1-59462-124-1*   *MSRP* **$29.95**

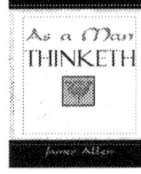

As a Man Thinketh
James Allen

"This little volume (the result of meditation and experience) is not intended as an exhaustive treatise on the much-written-upon subject of the power of thought. It is suggestive rather than explanatory, its object being to stimulate men and women to the discovery and perception of the truth that by virtue of the thoughts which they choose and encourage..."

Inspirational/Self Help   Pages:80

ISBN: *1-59462-231-0*   *MSRP* **$9.45**

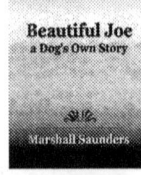

Beautiful Joe
Marshall Saunders

When Marshall visited the Moore family in 1892, she discovered Joe, a dog they had nursed back to health from his previous abusive home to live a happy life. So moved was she, that she wrote this classic masterpiece which won accolades and was recognized as a heartwarming symbol for humane animal treatment...

Fiction   Pages:256

ISBN: *1-59462-261-2*   *MSRP* **$18.45**

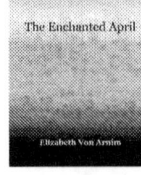

The Enchanted April
Elizabeth Von Arnim

It began in a woman's club in London on a February afternoon, an uncomfortable club, and a miserable afternoon. Mrs. Wilkins, who had come down from Hampstead to shop and had lunched at her club, took up The Times from the table in the smoking-room...

Fiction   Pages:368

ISBN: *1-59462-150-0*   *MSRP* **$23.45**

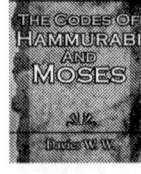

The Codes Of Hammurabi And
Moses - W. W. Davies

The discovery of the Hammurabi Code is one of the greatest achievements of archaeology, and is of paramount interest, not only to the student of the Bible, but also to all those interested in ancient history...

Religion   Pages:132

ISBN: *1-59462-338-4*   *MSRP* **$12.95**

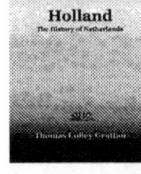

Holland - The History Of Netherlands
Thomas Colley Grattan

Thomas Grattan was a prestigious writer from Dublin who served as British Consul to the US. Among his works is an authoritative look at the history of Holland. A colorful and interesting look at history....

History/Politics   Pages:408

ISBN: *1-59462-137-3*   *MSRP* **$26.95**

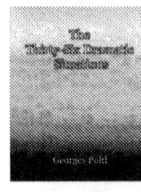

The Thirty-Six Dramatic Situations
Georges Polti

An incredibly useful guide for aspiring authors and playwrights. This volume categorizes every dramatic situation which could occur in a story and describes them in a list of 36 situations. A great aid to help inspire or formalize the creative writing process...

Self Help/Reference   Pages:204

ISBN: *1-59462-134-9*   *MSRP* **$15.95**

A Concise Dictionary of Middle English
A. L. Mayhew
Walter W. Skeat

The present work is intended to meet, in some measure, the requirements of those who wish to make some study of Middle-English, and who find a difficulty in obtaining such assistance as will enable them to find out the meanings and etymologies of the words most essential to their purpose...

Reference/History   Pages:332

ISBN: *1-59462-119-5*   *MSRP* **$29.95**

BOOK JUNGLE

Bringing Classics to Life

www.bookjungle.com *email: sales@bookjungle.com fax: 630-214-0564 mail: Book Jungle PO Box 2226 Champaign, IL 61825*

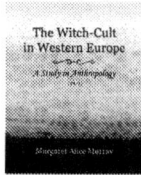

The Witch-Cult in Western Europe
Margaret Murray

The mass of existing material on this subject is so great that I have not attempted to make a survey of the whole of European "Witchcraft" but have confined myself to an intensive study of the cult in Great Britain. In order, however, to obtain a clearer understanding of the ritual and beliefs I have had recourse to French and Flemish sources...

Occult   **Pages:308**

ISBN: *1-59462-126-8*   **MSRP** *$22.45*

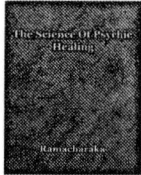

The Science Of Psychic Healing
Yogi Ramacharaka

This book is not a book of theories it deals with facts. Its author regards the best of theories as but working hypotheses to be used only until better ones present themselves. The "fact" is the principal thing the essential thing to uncover which the tool, theory, is used...

New Age/Health   **Pages:180**

ISBN: *1-59462-140-3*   **MSRP** *$13.95*

Bible Myths
Thomas Doane

In pursuing the study of the Bible Myths, facts pertaining thereto, in a condensed form, seemed to be greatly needed, and nowhere to be found. Widely scattered through hundreds of ancient and modern volumes, most of the contents of this book may indeed be found; but any previous attempt to trace exclusively the myths and legends...

Religion/History   **Pages:644**

ISBN: *1-59462-163-2*   **MSRP** *$38.95*

Tertium Organum
P. D. Ouspensky

A truly mind expanding writing that combines science with mysticism with unprecedented elegance. He presents the world we live in as a multi dimensional world and time as a motion through this world. But this isn't a cold and purely analytical explanation but a masterful presentation filled with similes and analogies...

New Age   **Pages:356**

ISBN: *1-59462-205-1*   **MSRP** *$23.95*

Advance Course in Yogi Philosophy
Yogi Ramacharaka

"The twelve lessons forming this volume were originally issued in the shape of monthly lessons, known as "The Advanced Course in Yogi Philosophy and Oriental Occultism" during a period of twelve months beginning with October, 1904, and ending September, 1905."

Philosophy/Inspirational/Self Help   **Pages:340**

ISBN: *1-59462-229-9*   **MSRP** *$22.95*

Ambassador Morgenthau's Story
Henry Morgenthau

"By this time the American people have probably become convinced that the Germans deliberately planned the conquest of the world. Yet they hesitate to convict on circumstantial evidence and for this reason all eye witnesses to this, the greatest crime in modern history, should volunteer their testimony..."

History   **Pages:472**

ISBN: *1-59462-244-2*   **MSRP** *$29.95*

The Aquarian Gospel of Jesus the Christ
Levi Dowling

A retelling of Jesus' story which tells us what happened during the twenty year gap left by the Bible's New Testament. It tells of his travels to the far-east where he studied with the masters and fought against the rigid caste system. This book has enjoyed a resurgence in modern America and provides spiritual insight with charm. Its influences can be seen throughout the Age of Aquarius.

Religion   **Pages:264**

ISBN: *1-59462-321-X*   **MSRP** *$18.95*

Philosophy Of Natural Therapeutics
Henry Lindlahr

We invite the earnest cooperation in this great work of all those who have awakened to the necessity for more rational living and for radical reform in healing methods...

Health/Philosophy/Self Help   **Pages:552**

ISBN: *1-59462-132-2*   **MSRP** *$34.95*

A Message to Garcia
Elbert Hubbard

This literary trifle, A Message to Garcia, was written one evening after supper, in a single hour. It was on the Twenty-second of February, Eighteen Hundred Ninety-nine, Washington's Birthday, and we were just going to press with the March Philistine...

New Age/Fiction   **Pages:92**

ISBN: *1-59462-144-6*   **MSRP** *$9.95*

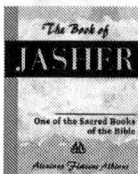

The Book of Jasher
Alcuinus Flaccus Albinus

The Book of Jasher is an historical religious volume that many consider as a missing holy book from the Old Testament. Particularly studied by the Church of Later Day Saints and historians, it covers the history of the world from creation until the period of Judges in Israel. It's authenticity is bolstered due to a reference to the Book of Jasher in the Bible in Joshua 10:13

Religion/History   **Pages:276**

ISBN: *1-59462-197-7*   **MSRP** *$18.95*

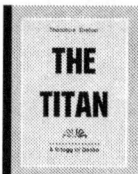

The Titan
Theodore Dreiser

"When Frank Algernon Cowperwood emerged from the Eastern District Penitentiary, in Philadelphia he realized that the old life he had lived in that city since boyhood was ended. His youth was gone, and with it had been lost the great business prospects of his earlier manhood. He must begin again..."

Fiction   **Pages:564**

ISBN: *1-59462-220-5*   **MSRP** *$33.95*

Biblical Essays
J. B. Lightfoot

About one-third of the present volume has already seen the light. The opening essay "On the Internal Evidence for the Authenticity and Genuineness of St John's Gospel" was published in the "Expositor" in the early months of 1890, and has been reprinted since...

Religion/History   **Pages:480**

ISBN: *1-59462-238-8*   **MSRP** *$30.95*

The Settlement Cook Book
Simon Kander

A legacy from the civil war, this book is a classic "American charity cookbook," which was used for fundraisers starting in Milwaukee. While it has transformed over the years, this printing provides great recipes from American history. Over two million copies have been sold. This volume contains a rich collection of recipes from noted chefs and hostesses of the turn of the century...

How-to   **Pages:472**

ISBN: *1-59462-256-6*   **MSRP** *$29.95*

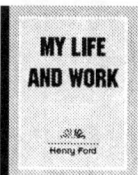

My Life and Work
Henry Ford

Henry Ford revolutionized the world with his implementation of mass production for the Model T automobile. Gain valuable business insight into his life and work with his own auto-biography... "We have only started on our development of our country we have not as yet, with all our talk of wonderful progress, done more than scratch the surface. The progress has been wonderful enough but..."

Biographies/History/Business   **Pages:300**

ISBN: *1-59462-198-5*   **MSRP** *$21.95*

www.bookjungle.com *email: sales@bookjungle.com fax: 630-214-0564 mail: Book Jungle PO Box 2226 Champaign, IL 61825*

QTY

The Rosicrucian Cosmo-Conception Mystic Christianity *by Max Heindel*   ISBN: *1-59462-188-8*   **$38.95**
The Rosicrucian Cosmo-conception is not dogmatic, neither does it appeal to any other authority than the reason of the student. It is; not controversial, but is; sent forth in the, hope that it may help to clear...   New Age/Religion Pages 646

Abandonment To Divine Providence *by Jean-Pierre de Caussade*   ISBN: *1-59462-228-0*   **$25.95**
"The Rev. Jean Pierre de Caussade was one of the most remarkable spiritual writers of the Society of Jesus in France in the 18th Century. His death took place at Toulouse in 1751. His works have gone through many editions and have been republished...   Inspirational/Religion Pages 400

Mental Chemistry *by Charles Haanel*   ISBN: *1-59462-192-6*   **$23.95**
Mental Chemistry allows the change of material conditions by combining and appropriately utilizing the power of the mind. Much like applied chemistry creates something new and unique out of careful combinations of chemicals the mastery of mental chemistry...   New Age Pages 354

The Letters of Robert Browning and Elizabeth Barret Barrett 1845-1846 vol II   ISBN: *1-59462-193-4*   **$35.95**
by Robert Browning and Elizabeth Barrett   Biographies Pages 596

Gleanings In Genesis (volume I) *by Arthur W. Pink*   ISBN: *1-59462-130-6*   **$27.45**
Appropriately has Genesis been termed "the seed plot of the Bible" for in it we have, in germ form, almost all of the great doctrines which are afterwards fully developed in the books of Scripture which follow...   Religion/Inspirational Pages 420

The Master Key *by L. W. de Laurence*   ISBN: *1-59462-001-6*   **$30.95**
In no branch of human knowledge has there been a more lively increase of the spirit of research during the past few years than in the study of Psychology, Concentration and Mental Discipline. The requests for authentic lessons in Thought Control, Mental Discipline and...   New Age/Business Pages 422

The Lesser Key Of Solomon Goetia *by L. W. de Laurence*   ISBN: *1-59462-092-X*   **$9.95**
This translation of the first book of the "Lemegton" which is now for the first time made accessible to students of Talismanic Magic was done, after careful collation and edition, from numerous Ancient Manuscripts in Hebrew, Latin, and French...   New Age/Occult Pages 92

Rubaiyat Of Omar Khayyam *by Edward Fitzgerald*   ISBN:*1-59462-332-5*   **$13.95**
Edward Fitzgerald, whom the world has already learned, in spite of his own efforts to remain within the shadow of anonymity, to look upon as one of the rarest poets of the century, was born at Bredfield, in Suffolk, on the 31st of March, 1809. He was the third son of John Purcell...   Music Pages 172

Ancient Law *by Henry Maine*   ISBN: *1-59462-128-4*   **$29.95**
The chief object of the following pages is to indicate some of the earliest ideas of mankind, as they are reflected in Ancient Law, and to point out the relation of those ideas to modern thought.   Religion/History Pages 452

Far-Away Stories *by William J. Locke*   ISBN: *1-59462-129-2*   **$19.45**
"Good wine needs no bush, but a collection of mixed vintages does. And this book is just such a collection. Some of the stories I do not want to remain buried for ever in the museum files of dead magazine-numbers an author's not unpardonable vanity..."   Fiction Pages 272

Life of David Crockett *by David Crockett*   ISBN: *1-59462-250-7*   **$27.45**
"Colonel David Crockett was one of the most remarkable men of the times in which he lived. Born in humble life, but gifted with a strong will, an indomitable courage, and unremitting perseverance...   Biographies/New Age Pages 424

Lip-Reading *by Edward Nitchie*   ISBN: *1-59462-206-X*   **$25.95**
Edward B. Nitchie, founder of the New York School for the Hard of Hearing, now the Nitchie School of Lip-Reading, Inc, wrote "LIP-READING Principles and Practice". The development and perfecting of this meritorious work on lip-reading was an undertaking...   How-to Pages 400

A Handbook of Suggestive Therapeutics, Applied Hypnotism, Psychic Science   ISBN: *1-59462-214-0*   **$24.95**
by Henry Munro   Health/New Age/Health/Self-help Pages 376

A Doll's House: and Two Other Plays *by Henrik Ibsen*   ISBN: *1-59462-112-8*   **$19.95**
Henrik Ibsen created this classic when in revolutionary 1848 Rome. Introducing some striking concepts in playwriting for the realist genre, this play has been studied the world over.   Fiction/Classics/Plays 308

The Light of Asia *by sir Edwin Arnold*   ISBN: *1-59462-204-3*   **$13.95**
In this poetic masterpiece, Edwin Arnold describes the life and teachings of Buddha. The man who was to become known as Buddha to the world was born as Prince Gautama of India but he rejected the worldly riches and abandoned the reigns of power when... Religion/History/Biographies Pages 170

The Complete Works of Guy de Maupassant *by Guy de Maupassant*   ISBN: *1-59462-157-8*   **$16.95**
"For days and days, nights and nights, I had dreamed of that first kiss which was to consecrate our engagement, and I knew not on what spot I should put my lips..."   Fiction/Classics Pages 240

The Art of Cross-Examination *by Francis L. Wellman*   ISBN: *1-59462-309-0*   **$26.95**
Written by a renowned trial lawyer, Wellman imparts his experience and uses case studies to explain how to use psychology to extract desired information through questioning.   How-to/Science/Reference Pages 408

Answered or Unanswered? *by Louisa Vaughan*   ISBN: *1-59462-248-5*   **$10.95**
Miracles of Faith in China   Religion Pages 112

The Edinburgh Lectures on Mental Science (1909) *by Thomas*   ISBN: *1-59462-008-3*   **$11.95**
This book contains the substance of a course of lectures recently given by the writer in the Queen Street Hall, Edinburgh. Its purpose is to indicate the Natural Principles governing the relation between Mental Action and Material Conditions...   New Age/Psychology Pages 148

Ayesha *by H. Rider Haggard*   ISBN: *1-59462-301-5*   **$24.95**
Verily and indeed it is the unexpected that happens! Probably if there was one person upon the earth from whom the Editor of this, and of a certain previous history, did not expect to hear again...   Classics Pages 380

Ayala's Angel *by Anthony Trollope*   ISBN: *1-59462-352-X*   **$29.95**
The two girls were both pretty; but Lucy who was twenty-one who supposed to be simple and comparatively unattractive, whereas Ayala was credited, as her Bombwhat romantic name might show, with poetic charm and a taste for romance. Ayala when her father died was nineteen...   Fiction Pages 484

The American Commonwealth *by James Bryce*   ISBN: *1-59462-286-8*   **$34.45**
An interpretation of American democratic political theory. It examines political mechanics and society from the perspective of Scotsman James Bryce   Politics Pages 572

Stories of the Pilgrims *by Margaret P. Pumphrey*   ISBN: *1-59462-116-0*   **$17.95**
This book explores pilgrims religious oppression in England as well as their escape to Holland and eventual crossing to America on the Mayflower, and their early days in New England...   History Pages 268

BOOK JUNGLE

Bringing Classics to Life

www.bookjungle.com *email: sales@bookjungle.com fax: 630-214-0564 mail: Book Jungle PO Box 2226 Champaign, IL 61825*

QTY

The Fasting Cure *by Sinclair Upton*   ISBN: *1-59462-222-1*   **$13.95**
In the Cosmopolitan Magazine for May, 1910, and in the Contemporary Review (London) for April, 1910, I published an article dealing with my experiences in fasting. I have written a great many magazine articles, but never one which attracted so much attention...   New Age/Self Help/Health Pages 164

Hebrew Astrology *by Sepharial*   ISBN: *1-59462-308-2*   **$13.45**
In these days of advanced thinking it is a matter of common observation that we have left many of the old landmarks behind and that we are now pressing forward to greater heights and to a wider horizon than that which represented the mind-content of our progenitors...   Astrology Pages 144

Thought Vibration or The Law of Attraction in the Thought World   ISBN: *1-59462-127-6*   **$12.95**
by William Walker Atkinson   Psychology/Religion Pages 144

Optimism *by Helen Keller*   ISBN: *1-59462-108-X*   **$15.95**
Helen Keller was blind, deaf, and mute since 19 months old, yet famously learned how to overcome these handicaps, communicate with the world, and spread her lectures promoting optimism. An inspiring read for everyone...   Biographies/Inspirational Pages 84

Sara Crewe *by Frances Burnett*   ISBN: *1-59462-360-0*   **$9.45**
In the first place, Miss Minchin lived in London. Her home was a large, dull, tall one, in a large, dull square, where all the houses were alike, and all the sparrows were alike, and where all the door-knockers made the same heavy sound...   Childrens/Classic Pages 88

The Autobiography of Benjamin Franklin *by Benjamin Franklin*   ISBN: *1-59462-135-7*   **$24.95**
The Autobiography of Benjamin Franklin has probably been more extensively read than any other American historical work, and no other book of its kind has had such ups and downs of fortune. Franklin lived for many years in England, where he was agent...   Biographies/History Pages 332

Name	
Email	
Telephone	
Address	
City, State ZIP	

☐ **Credit Card**   ☐ **Check / Money Order**

Credit Card Number	
Expiration Date	
Signature	

Please Mail to: Book Jungle
PO Box 2226
Champaign, IL 61825
or Fax to: 630-214-0564

ORDERING INFORMATION

web*: www.bookjungle.com*
email*: sales@bookjungle.com*
fax*: 630-214-0564*
mail*: Book Jungle PO Box 2226 Champaign, IL 61825*
or PayPal *to sales@bookjungle.com*

Please contact us for bulk discounts

DIRECT-ORDER TERMS

**20% Discount if You Order
Two or More Books**
Free Domestic Shipping!
Accepted: Master Card, Visa,
Discover, American Express